CREATIVE SUFFERING

THE RIPPLE OF HOPE

CREATIVE SUFFERING

THE RIPPLE OF HOPE

Alan Paton
John Howard Griffin
Frederick Franck
Glenn T. Seaborg
Charles Davis
John L. McKenzie, S.J.
Frank J. Sheed
Herbert Richardson

Pilgrim Press & *The National Catholic Reporter*

PHOTOGRAPHS:

PAGE 70	Camera Press-Pix
PAGE 106	Paul Koby, Cambridge, Mass.
PAGE 56	USAEC PHOTO by J. E. Westcott
PAGE 12	Courtesy of Annie Laurie Williams
PAGE 24	George Curtsinger, 1401 South Main St., Fort Worth, Texas
PAGE 96	Courtesy of Sheed & Ward, Inc., New York
PAGE 38	Ruigrok, Volkskrant.

Creative Suffering: The Ripple of Hope is a copublishing project of Pilgrim Press, the trade imprint of United Church Press, Philadelphia, Pennsylvania, and *The National Catholic Reporter,* Kansas City, Missouri.

Library of Congress Catalog Card Number 79–106559

SBN 8298-0152-9

Contents

Introduction

Like every creative effort, this book has its flesh and blood context. It grew from an idea to reality in the aftermath of the assassinations of Martin Luther King Jr. and Robert F. Kennedy. The time was one of stunned shock at the vehemence of the violence of America, a violence experienced on all fronts: in the cities and in Vietnam.

The responses to this violence have in turn been creative and destructive, ranging from an outpouring of new resolves, art, idealism, and hope, to more blood, death, and fire.

This book attempts to spotlight a core thought of Martin Luther King Jr.'s theology: redemptive suffering. In an age when there is real self-consciousness about most traditional theological themes, the authors—in the main nontheologians—explore suffering in its broadest meaning and find it a creative, human force that can change society and can bring hope. Their subject is not the morbid or the syrupy pious. Rather, the suffering they talk of is that of the politician, the artist, the scientist. They highlight the creative suffering which is the responsibility of everyman: the willing acceptance of the vulnerability and risk that comes to the man or woman who expresses an unpopular view, who works for peace and justice. That a growing number of people accept this suffering has been evident in the past year, especially in the peace movement.

Creative Suffering: The Ripple of Hope is the response, then, of the editors of *The National Catholic Reporter* to a central need of our American society. These essays, which first appeared as a lenten series in *The National Catholic Reporter,* are a tribute to all those who stand up, assume responsibility, and thereby, in Robert Kennedy's words, create ripples of hope which converge in mighty force.

James F. Andrews
Managing Editor
The National Catholic Reporter

In addition to his political activity as president of the Liberal Party in South Africa, Alan Paton has won world-wide fame as a writer. He is best known in the United States for his *Cry, the Beloved Country!* and for his essays in *Saturday Review*.

1

Alan Paton

Why Suffering?

The "problem of suffering" has exercised the minds of men for centuries, especially the minds of those who want to believe that God is father as well as creator. Why does he permit pain and suffering to exist? Why didn't he make the world good and kind and peaceful? Why didn't he make men who would not hurt or destroy in all that holy mountain? Was the world worth making, and is life worth living, with its Vietnam and its Nigeria, its cancer and arthritis, its decay of personal meaning and privacy, and the hopeless gloom of lonely and disillusioned old age?

These aren't easy questions to answer. I certainly hate to be asked them at a party. How is one to explain how evil got into the universe if one doesn't believe in the devil? Is one to believe that God the Savior came to Bethlehem to make reparation for the cruelty of God the Creator? Or is one to believe that suffering, like man himself, is a product of a blind evolutionary process that produces orderliness by accident?

I can't accept any of these answers, but I can't produce others. My intellect cannot cope with the problem of suffering, nor can it accept the speculations of other intellects, which I feel are speculating out of their range and capacity. These are questions that cannot be answered in an article or a book, but only in a life.

I have a friend who has had both her breasts removed, and has now developed cancer of the spine, but her conversation is one of continual thanks to God and her friends and her neighbors and her woman servant. What is it that she knows? What has she found out? She has certainly not found out the answers to these difficult questions, but she has certainly found a meaning for her life. In some way she has taken her suffering and made it her instrument, the use of which has given her this continual thankfulness, and has given her friends a shining example of faith and courage and love. I don't think she did it by an act of will. I think that's the way she was heading. She was predisposed, when she was struck down, to accept her affliction as an instrument.

This kind of victory seems to presuppose this kind of predisposition, but one should not be dogmatic about that, because the sudden or gradual onslaught of an affliction causes profound changes in the personality. At one extreme the doubters begin to believe and the careless begin to be careful. At the other extreme are those who go from believing to not-believing, and from not-believing to not-hoping, from confidence to despair.

I know another woman, who, because her teen-age daughter suddenly threw off home discipline and conventional morality, lost her own faith. What went wrong? Why was her faith, which outwardly appeared unshakable, not able to withstand this blow? Was her belief in the goodness of God contingent on her own good luck?

All who are mature, whether young or old, accept suffering as inseparable from life; even if it is not experienced, the possibility of it is always there. I myself cannot conceive of life without suffering. I cannot even conceive that life could have meaning without suffering. There would certainly be no music, no theater, no literature, no art. I suspect that the alternative to a universe in which there is suffering, in which evil struggles with good and cruelty with mercy, would be a universe of nothingness, where there would be neither good nor evil, no happiness, only an eternity of uninterrupted banality.

If my suspicion is true, then I vote for the universe we have, where we have our joy that has been made real by our suffering, as the silence of the night is made real by the sounds of the night. And we have our suffering there too, made real by our joy. Such a multifold universe, such a multifold life, despite all the unanswerable questions that they raise, seem more consonant with the idea of a creative and imaginative God than any garden of Eden.

If suffering is an inescapable part of life, what does one do about it? There are many ways of reacting to it, but only one that is profitable, and that is to accept it, and use it, and where possible, to prevent it, alleviate it, bring it to an end.

When Francis of Assisi got down from his horse and

embraced the leper, he solved the problem of suffering for himself. And what was more, he was later able to accept and use his own suffering, and to sing his way to death. He did not curse leprosy, nor did he curse God for making or allowing leprosy; he got down from his horse and kissed the leper. This act changed his whole life, and the lives of countless thousands of others. From that time onward, lepers became for Francis what the untouchables became for Gandhi—*Narijans,* "the children of God." What was loathsome and terrifying became a source of sweetness and strength. Francis wrote in his will, "The Lord himself led me among them, and I showed mercy to them, and when I left them, what had seemed bitter to me was changed into sweetness of body and soul."

Although I have contemplated this miracle for many years, it has never ceased to fill me with wonder. For in that moment Francis shed all doubt and anxiety and uncertainty, and all grief over the unsolvable mystery of pain and evil and sorrow, and put himself and his life into God's hands to be made the instrument of God's peace, so that he might ease pain and conquer evil and give comfort and strength to the sorrowful. He was no longer one to suffer and endure, he was one to love and to do.

One must straightway admit that one can only do this if one has the conviction that God is the father of all mankind, and that he cares for all his creatures. But this does not deny fullness of life to those who do not have this conviction, yet desire to be an instrument of some unknown but good power. Once we make ourselves the instruments of such a power, the grip of melancholy and doubt begins to loosen, even in our present restless and unhappy world.

We no longer agonize over the problem of suffering, we make of ourselves instruments for its alleviation. It is almost as though we said to God, "Some say you are cruel, and we confess that the cruelty of the world troubles us, so that we have moments of doubt; but of your goodness we have no doubt, having seen it in the life of Jesus, therefore we put our lives in your hands, so that you may use them for the sake of others." This is, so far as I know, the only way in which one can solve for oneself the problem of suffering.

Jesus accepted evil and suffering as being "in the nature of things." He said "it must needs be that offenses come." Paul wrote of the whole creation groaning and travailing in pain until now. I do not pretend to be able to interpret these sayings, but it is clear that both Jesus and his great disciple accepted this wound in the creation, and having accepted it, devoted their lives to the healing of it.

That is the creative act, not to ask who dealt this wound to the creation, not to accuse God of having dealt it, but to make of one's life an instrument of God's peace. This act is doubly creative, in that it transforms both giver and receiver, and indeed it can be said of many of us that one of our deepest experiences of God is in this act of giving and receiving.

Up till now I have been writing of that kind of suffering which we are helpless to prevent. If it afflicts others, then we can become the bearers of comfort and strength, if not of healing. If it afflicts ourselves, we may by our acceptance of it also become the bearers of comfort and strength to others.

There is also the kind of suffering that we bring on

ourselves through acts of negligence and indulgence, and it is closely akin to the first, and must be accepted in the same way if it is to be creative. But there is a different kind of suffering altogether, when we suffer at the hands of authority or society or our neighbors, because of what we do and say and believe for reasons of conscience. This is a kind of suffering that can be—though it is not always so—highly creative. Some of us believe that society cannot be made whole without it. This suffering compounded with joy is the gospel, so that men and women take with willingness a road that may lead them to death and the cross.

It seems to me that there is a growing eagerness among Christians to rediscover the gospel, and a growing readiness to accept the compound of suffering and joy, and a growing comprehension that the gospel story is as relevant to life today as it has ever been. If it appears irrelevant, that is because it has been so heavily overlaid by pieties, observances, and prohibitions, that no one can get at it anymore. God has been locked into the church, into its dogmas and doctrines, and the sense of his omnipresence has been lost.

Man has always been torn between saving himself and giving himself, and Christian man has never found it easy to believe that it is only by giving himself that he can save himself. He finds it hard, even bitter, to accept that being saved is only a consequence, and that it is the consequence of having given. He used to ask the question, and with great urgency: "Am I saved?" whereas the real question should have been: "Am I giving?"

In my own country of South Africa, it is a matter of

great importance to a white South African to be saved, to be safe, to be secure, to have some future in a country in which he is so heavily outnumbered. This desire to be saved, to be secure, is a dominant desire, and the majority of white Christians simply cannot believe that one achieves security by giving. Yet they desire to remain Christians, therefore they create a pseudo-gospel which enables them to save themselves and give themselves simultaneously. One of our foremost statesmen put it categorically, that the prime duty of a Christian is to look after himself, because if Christians don't look after themselves, what will become of Christianity?

When I write that there is a growing eagerness among Christians to rediscover the gospel, I do not mean that this applies to all Christians; and because it does not apply to all Christians, it follows that there is developing a new cleavage in the church, not along denominational lines, but between those who are rediscovering the gospel and those who believe, either that there is nothing to rediscover, or that it is subversive and communistic or just plain heretical to want to rediscover it. This cleavage is apparent in all denominations, so that a new and odd and exciting kind of ecumenicity is appearing.

This rediscovering of the gospel is dangerous in South Africa, for the authorities don't want it rediscovered. They want it to stay as it is, because they want the country to stay as it is. Apartheid and the gospel are more or less the same thing, and anyone who doesn't believe in Apartheid is really not believing in the gospel. What is more, anyone who disbelieves strongly enough, anyone who exposes the cruelties of Apartheid, anyone who is too active or too vocal in his opposition to Apartheid, will be dealt with severely. His right to move about and communicate and seek employment will be drastically restricted, usually for a period of five years. And if at the end of that time he is not prepared to change radically his manner of opposition, these restrictions will be reimposed, usually for a further five years.

I write with authority about this, not because it has happened to me (I have suffered only in respect to my passport), but because it has happened to many of my friends. Their trouble was that they took too seriously the injunction to "seek judgment." They understood clearly that to seek judgment was to invite suffering, and they decided to go on seeking judgment. Not one of them would have changed his or her course to avoid suffering.

This is suffering at its most creative. It changed no laws, it softened no customs, but it made the country a better place to live in. What was a land of fear, they made a land of courage also. Not only did they help and encourage others, but they acquired a strength that could withstand all the assaults of the enemy. To put it in religious language, they made themselves instruments of the divine creativity.

It is interesting to note that as one writes about these matters, one writes only incidentally about suffering. And that is as it should be. One is not really writing about suffering, one is writing about living, about loving, about giving. One is writing about the discovery that you cannot—I don't know if this is true of all societies—live and love and give without suffering. But your purpose is to live and love and give, and if suffering is part of the price to be paid, then you pay it. One does not seek suffering, one seeks judgment.

To me one of the most stirring stories of martyrdom is that of Hugh Latimer, who knew well that support for the Reformation might lead him to death. Shortly after Mary, daughter of Henry VIII, came to the throne, he was summoned to appear at Westminster, and though he could have escaped, he obeyed joyfully. On October 16, 1555, he and Ridley were led to the stake at Oxford. He greeted Ridley with the words: "Be of good comfort, Master Ridley, and play the man; we shall this day light such a candle by God's grace in England as I trust shall never be put out." He then "received the flame (as it were) embracing it. After he had stroked his face with his hands, and (as it were) bathed them a little in the fire, he soon died (as it appeared) with very little pain or none." He died thus without fear, he had had a life to live, and if the price for living it was to be burned alive, then of course one must be burned alive.

The world is now passing through a phase—which one hopes will soon end—where the state takes to itself greater and greater powers over the lives of its citizens. In some countries (mine is one) it has taken to itself the power to punish without recourse to the courts of law. In some countries (mine is one) a citizen can be held incommunicado for an indefinite period (or a fixed period that can be repeated indefinitely), and will only be released when his answers to questions are "satisfactory" to the authorities.

In my country, if an African man goes to work in a "white" area (and there is very little work in any other kind of area), then he may not take his wife and family with him. One could quote a thousand more examples of the power and indifference of the state, but the question I am asking is this: What does a Christian do, what does a good citizen do, who is seeking judgment, relieving the oppressed, judging the fatherless, pleading for the widow?

There is only one answer for the Christian who has come, often reluctantly, often fearfully, to the belief that the cross is not just for Good Friday. He must, in spite of the anger of the state, in spite very often of the anger of his neighbors, stand up for the right, and speak it and do it if he can. Quite apart from what he does for himself, which is considerable, he kindles hope in the breasts of many people, who see in him a living proof that the world was worth making, and is worth living in after all. Fortunate is society when those who love it are alive to its faults, and ready to spend their lives in its service. Because that is what living really means.

No one ever brought greater suffering on the world than Hitler. He shook man's faith in the goodness of life and of man. Yet what evil he inflicted with his absolute power was atoned for by men and women without power at all, who died rather than yield to him, and who left us the imperishable legacy of their letters written just before death. They changed no laws, they did not prevent the world from plunging into disaster, yet they restored man's faith in the goodness of life and of man. You cannot be more creative than that.

John Howard Griffin, author and photographer, is a student of primitive cultures and intergroup and intercultural relationships. His works include *Devil Rides Outside, Land of the High Sky,* and *Black Like Me*. For *Black Like Me,* he received the Anisfield Wolf Award of the *Saturday Review*. His personal experience of his subject overflows the third person genre he has chosen in this article.

2

John Howard Griffin

The Terrain of Physical Pain

All men know something of physical pain. Great or small, it is part of lived experience. Some men are called to experience suffering deeply and for prolonged periods, to become familiar with its modes and its nuances within themselves. Such men traverse a terrain that goes from the known to the mysterious, each at his own speed of perception.

Science can tell the sufferer much about the causes of pain and some of its effects and perhaps some of its remedies. Each sufferer's inventiveness shows him ways of adapting to his limitations. At first it is hard, concrete. The sufferer comes to know what is known, learns to do what must be done. But soon, with growing experience, these things fade into the area of the mechanical. Then new and vague truths begin to emerge, truths difficult to formulate, and the sufferer perceives that much of what he experiences, much that is most profound in his experience, simply lies beyond the realm of ideas. For this reason, I think, speculative explanations of suffering often sound false, off-key to the sufferer because they rarely conform to his own lived reality.

Certainly every sufferer has had the experience of having his condition "explained" to him by people who have had only superficial experience with pain, which is rather like explaining the keyboard to a concert pianist. Nothing is more ironic to the man steeped in physical pain than to be told by the visitor, pink-cheeked with health, that the sufferer is "God's pet," or that God has allowed him "the deep privilege of suffering," even though these things may have some truth in them.

On the other hand, those who have known pain profoundly are the ones most wary of uttering the clichés about suffering. Experience with the mystery takes one beyond the realm of ideas and produces finally a kind of muteness or at least a reticence to express in words the solace that can only be expressed by an attitude of union with the sufferer.

"In these terrible sufferings," Raïssa Maritain wrote in her journals for 1934, "I am able to be sustained somewhat by the processes of tenderness and friendship. Indeed, no fine reasoning could have the same effect. This explains the complaints of Job against his friends who reasoned, however, perfectly well." And she went on to speak of "This faculty to act at once on two planes—that of concrete experience, demanding and painful, and that of an abstract and liberating conception rooted in the same experience. It has been this for me, and this permits me to live."

In this faculty to act at once on two planes, the French poet went to the heart of the mystery. It is this concept that comes to some sufferers to transform the energies of pain into profoundly creative energies. These may never show themselves in tangible forms, but the intangible effects of creativity are at least as important in the resonances they produce as the tangible ones.

This faculty to act at once on two planes can be dissipated when it becomes merely an attempt to escape an awareness of pain. No, it must be the contrary—an acceptance and an awareness of the reality that exists in pain and that sometimes becomes obsessive in pain, and then a growing ability, from the same root, to stand off and become the observer; and then again, passing on to the observation of other things until at length and in the natural order of things, the observing self comes to the realization that self, even in pain, is less interesting than other objects of contemplation. It is this realization, which takes time, that ultimately liberates the sufferer: not from his suffering, no; not from an acute awareness of his suffering, no; but from the otherwise exclusive, obsessive, paralyzing, sterilizing enslavement of suffering.

This begins to occur, for example, when the man who is deprived of some freedom by pain—perhaps the freedom to walk—is initially overwhelmed by the deprivation: absorbed in the deprivation or the pain; then, as he learns, as he lives with it, the interest is less sustained. He can see the person not thus deprived climb steps without any hesitancy and feel some unwholeness because he cannot do that; but then he can begin to see that simple act which to him is now impossible no longer as a reproach to himself, no longer as a reminder of his own deprivation. But in the light of that, from the same root, as a marvelous sight, he sees the man bounding up steps as something extraordinary, beautiful; he sees and marvels at the freedom and lack of pain and concern in the man climbing the steps, and this rather than his own inability is far more interesting. He watches, and feels a kind of joy that others can do this marvelous thing. He watches it the way others might watch a great athlete, or a dancer like Nureyev: not in self-loathing because few men are great athletes or have the skills of a Nureyev, but because of the beauty of those who have these gifts.

The sufferer can come to this secret realization: he can view those who do not suffer almost as though they were great artworks, with his own special lights and perceptions, with his own special astonishment. This is not a question really of generosity, but of a deep natural priority of interest. He has begun to perceive that self is less interesting than what is interesting; he has come to learn the difference between what is merely average and what is normal. By the average, he is a deprived and afflicted being, but when this becomes his own normalcy, then the average is simply viewed by him as extraordinary. From this can spring a truth that confuses those who know little of suffering: the core of joy that lies at the heart of even the most intense suffering; the supreme activity of wisdom that does not need movement.

There are few road maps, and there should be few, to guide a man who faces suffering as a new experience. The way ahead is essentially unknown for each sufferer and because of the individuality of each human person the way has to be clarified through his own experience. This can cause great fears at the outset. It can cause a man to play roles, to assume masks of bravery, courage, patience, even when such masks are alien to the reality the sufferer experiences within himself. Because he is in unfamiliar territory, the sufferer naturally assumes attitudes he thinks society expects and admires. Before suffering itself can clarify values for him, he begins to search frantically for the reasons for his suffering.

"I suppose God does not let suffering evaporate uselessly," Pierre Reverdy wrote in a letter to his friend Stanislas Fumet, "and we can contribute to the good, no matter how incredible that might seem to us, whenever God decides."

Some men grasp this kind of concept as a salvaging one at the outset of prolonged suffering. In searching for the "why," men can be driven to accept this as a reason. Men can cling to this concept as an act of faith. Men can offer up suffering and find some sense in it if it "can contribute to the good." Some men simply cannot. I suspect that to every man who passes into this kind of experience this whole concept, even when it is accepted blindly on faith, is highly dubious, because what is happening to the body, to the rational animal is not really rational: assaults are taking place that the rational mind cannot understand. The mind seeks reasons for what is happening to the body, and so the mind grasps at these "reasons" even while the body casts them into doubt. The body can even lead men to suspect that there are no reasons, that it just happened, that the pain is going to "evaporate uselessly."

Only later, and usually in ways quite different from the expected or hoped-for ones, does the realization come that a transformation has occurred—a massive transformation—the effects of which begin to manifest themselves even while the causes remain obscure; and the man who has suffered deeply can see in these effects that nothing was, in fact, wasted.

Lionel Trilling once observed that culture is a prison unless we know the key that unlocks the door. He referred to those learned behavior patterns inculcated in men from earliest childhood according to the customs and traditions of culture, patterns so deeply inculcated that men tend to call them "human nature," which they are not at all. Man's individuality is frequently blunted by the process, which seeks to make men of the same culture resemble one another. The saints have always struggled against this, seeking a reality that transcends cultural limitations and delusions.

One of the things discovered first by those entering into suffering as adults is this contradiction between cultural concepts and the reality that physical pain imposes. Usually this enters the door of humiliation, making such a man aware of his clays, clarifying the tendency to deny (or hide) the animality of his physical self. For in pain, it is the animal self that calls attention.

In a society or culture that has placed great emphasis on "the more and less decent parts" of the body, in which spiritual writers have viewed the body as an impediment, sometimes even the enemy, to spiritual growth, it has been inevitable that men come to delusions about themselves, to want to show God only those more "decent aspects"—in other words, to drift toward an angelism where they see as contemptible those things about themselves that the creator obviously saw as good: the animal functioning that is part of man.

The delusion is particularly dangerous because it exists at profound and unconscious levels. It is through this delusion that men still widely believe that man grows spiritually by truncating his humanity rather than by perfecting it. Such men, called to pain, perhaps discover for the first time (and with what a sense of relief) that when man is stretched out in pain before God and before man, in all his nakedness and vulnerability, there are no "more or less decent" parts, and he can become reconciled to that from which he should never have been alienated in the first place. His reality shows him, too, that many of the values he has been taught are blessedly untrue: the idea of strength as a necessary virtue, for example, crashes when a man becomes helpless through physical suffering and has to allow his body to be handled and cared for like that of a child.

The man strapped naked to a table and turned in all directions, even upside down, for a spinal myelitis examination, aware and in initial embarrassment because doctors and nurses are observing him, not only in his nakedness but especially in his very defenselessness, comes to realize that what he has hidden (intellectually, mentally) was not really hidden. It is still there in his suffering body, and finally he has to face it; but simultaneously he has to recognize something far more important: those "strangers" who view his body and handle it, do so in the profound charity of a search for healing. No matter how physically and psychologically painful this may be, he can realize that those who help are lifted to charity through the pain that afflicts his body. For that amount of time, something tremendous and pure has occurred. And he may even feel the deep balm of a first understanding that the body, so denied in some of its aspects, so hated, perhaps, has longed for the same sunlight as the soul; and that in God's sight, if not in man's, there is no blushing, no turning away, no priorities in parts but a reality of the whole.

In another sense, again at levels of pure resonance, once a sufferer can come into intimacy with his suffering, he can come to a deeper perception: the denial of cultural concepts that have led to the belief that fellow human beings if they belong to other cultures, are in fact intrinsically and fundamentally *different.* Pain is universal. In learning this the sufferer finds himself united to universal suffering. Every man who lives, regardless of his cultural or ethnic differences, faces the identical human problems of loving, of suffering, of dying. In the isolation of pain, the sufferer faces these realities and gradually realizes that pain in the body can cure things which are not the body, that it brings clarity to intuitions, unclouds perceptions, and opens up the whole area of intuitive knowledge known as "prephilosophy" that can replace cultural distortions with a reality before which such distortions can no longer stand.

"In the realm of the spirit, it is not so much what we do as what we allow to be done to us," Gerald Vann once wrote. Certainly, at the deepest levels of human creativity, a part of genius has been the ability of men to allow themselves to be used as a sort of filter for experience; to accept the experience imposed on them without even judging its value, allowing it to enter, allowing it to teach, and then letting it come back out in some form of expression —prayer, silence, music, contemplation, art.

Certain great masterworks are otherwise unexplainable in human terms: some of the poems of St. John of the Cross, the Mozart G Minor Quintet, the great Opus 132 Quartet of Beethoven, to mention only a few. In these, experience, often in the form of intense suffering, has been accepted, handled, then released. As Reverdy pointed out, great works tend to happen despite men rather than because of some purely human initiative. "We have to believe that what happens despite us is better than what we do on our own," he wrote.

The sufferer, because he really has no alternative, is forced finally by his suffering to recognize this core truth: things are being done to him. Values he once held are crumbling. Only later, perhaps, will he see that such values are replaced by others. In a society with a mania for organization and a consequent mania for demanding that every action produce a measurable result, he begins to learn that results in themselves are a needless luxury. He may even learn an ultimate wisdom—not to care about results, not to waste his time looking for them—submitting himself to the action and allowing the results to take care of themselves, in the knowledge that if "God does not allow suffering to evaporate uselessly," then that suffering is being used and how really does not matter. If suffering does evaporate uselessly, then nothing the sufferer can do is going to change that.

He senses a tremendous liberation from such values.

He trusts his humanity which he begins to sense in a personal and individual way. "The world needs to see results; I don't," he says. Involved in pain, knowing it intimately, he no longer looks on pain as the feared stranger even when it remains in fact the unwanted companion. From his perspective he learns that others fear this unknown, that others suffer in his sufferings, perhaps even more tormentedly because they do not know them with any precision. He learns pity for those who do not suffer but must witness his suffering. The sufferer then takes on the role of consoling those who are spared. When this is achieved, he can offer true solace and can stop being concerned about "playing the brave sufferer."

Very simply then, physical suffering, if the sufferer allows it to do with him what it can—in a kind of simplicity and openness to its teachings—turns the sufferer into giver, into lover, into consoler. Long experience with physical suffering has taught him that he can bear what he has borne. But he cannot bear it when others suffer. It constantly reawakens him to mercy and to an authentic pity which bring in their wake a melting of the callouses of indifference and unconcern for others. Even the man totally immobilized and locked in pain, *the moment all elements of self-pity have evaporated,* can spread an authentic and curative pity that sometimes seems to blaze from him.

And this is the plane where his paths of experience join the paths of men of the spirit—here he has been driven into the desert, isolated. "A too-great affliction places a human being beneath pity, provokes disgust, horror, and scorn," wrote Simone Weil. No matter how surrounded by men, the sufferer is sometimes isolated, a hermit in the desert of his suffering. Whereas the mystic, the contemplative seeks the desert, the solitude, the essences of reality; the sufferer is taken there by his suffering. Men fear the deserts; men want the security of shelter, of walls, of companionship with people; for who can bear the terrible vastness of too great a view of creation?

The desert, the silence, the solitude—the sufferer is placed there and has to look, has to face the whole of his experience, has to face the infinite. And like the desert dweller, he has to expand with it until it is no longer terror but solace he finds there. He communicates, and more, he can soon realize that even when pain so diffuses his faculties that he cannot utter a single verbal prayer, the pain itself can become the most eloquent of all prayers and he need not preoccupy himself with that. In "allowing to be done to him" he begins to understand Cassian's statement that there is no perfect prayer if the religious perceives that he is praying. The prayer of pain, the gift of pain.

The sufferer, in his own time, finds himself a great distance from former concepts where he felt he had to offer God and the world something grand, something beautiful and lustrous, something "worthy." He knows now that the great secret is simply not to withhold anything, not to withhold even wretchedness if that is all one has.

There are limits to the joy as well as to the suffering that human beings can bear—so these glimpses into realities beyond the realm of ideas are transitory. However, once experienced, they alter everything from then on. They change the individual. He is no longer average. They become part of the deep originality of the human individual.

These are secret things to the sufferer. If he has entered deeply into this special solitude, he feels words cheapen and distort it. Thus the sufferer sometimes tries to hide his suffering from the public gaze, feels uncomfortable when men talk of his "witness," not because of modesty but because men try to use liberating truths in an arrangement that re-imprisons them in what are merely cultural values. No, these are private things. They become other things when the sufferer is called on to reveal them. We remember the mystic's cry when deprived of solitude by men who wanted his wisdom: "I seek God and you surround me only with religion."

The ultimate and true effects of suffering can only occur, from the sufferer's viewpoint, in the very silence and solitude from which they spring, beyond the realm of ideas. These effects—wisdom, giving, mercy, love—produce their own ferment. The man who has allowed these realities to come to him through the experience of suffering, in their own time and with their own priorities, knows that somehow and without any special action of his own initiative the ferment of these effects will be returned to the world in some form which is ultimately redemptive. He himself, henceforth and forever, if he has been deeply enough wounded, will remain reawakened to mercy and to that whole mysterious cycle of replenishment in which he has allowed himself to be used, to be an instrument, a filter.

Finally, to his own great astonishment, he will experience within himself the effects of his mercy, effects that he never desired, never expected. This is what Gerald Vann understood so deeply when he wrote: "The merciful shall obtain more than they can desire. How is that? Because pity enlarges the heart, and where there is infinite pity, there is infinite enlargement of the heart, and so an infinite capacity for joy—and what that joy is, no man can tell."

Dr. Frederick Franck is best known for his drawings of the Second Vatican Council and Pope John. He has authored several books, including *The Exploding Church,* and his work appears regularly in *New Yorker* magazine.

3

Frederick Franck

Victories and Defeats on Paper

If I am to write with any meaning at all about the artist's despair and hope, I must literally undress in public. Not being a habitual stripper, this worries me, especially since I have neither sensational bust nor gorgeous legs to show. Not that I believe in "gorgeous legs." I have drawn too many thousands of legs. I have learned that only in nylon and high heels are they glamorous, these stilts for locomotion. The machinery of the knee, the pale veins under the skin, educe contemplation, compassion rather than agitation.

If I were to write objectively or intellectually I might as well say nothing. So I must speak subjectively, even at the risk of being charged with self-dramatization, for I ask to be believed if I say that for me, a grown man, between the seeing of an apple tree or a face and drawing it with my pen so that it becomes true to my vision, there often lies agony. I must become that tree, that face, while I am drawing or I fail . . .

At the same time I realize how absurd it may sound to the rational citizen, this confession of finding one's victories over life as well as one's defeats on a piece of paper or canvas. And *that* regardless of success and recognition! Is it more or less absurd than to manufacture lipstick, cola, or napalm—for profit?

Moreover, I feel I am not really speaking as "the artist," "the writer" at all, but as a man who draws and paints and writes some of his mortal time. I have indeed done hundreds of paintings and thousands of drawings, I have had exhibitions, have written a few books. Still, if you ask me, "What are you?" I hesitate to describe myself as "the artist," "the writer." Hell, I have been doctor, dentist, husband, father, builder, lover, teacher! In private—and therefore in this confession—I laugh at these labels, as I do at religious labels, because all these labels are lies, masks, the moment you stick them onto yourself. Let others do it if they must! While I am writing, I am a writer, while I am doctoring a doctor, while painting a painter. The moment I neither draw nor paint nor write, I feel hardly a man, let alone "the artist." I am a miserable cur, worthless, impotent, despicable.

I admire and am jealous of any car mechanic, checkgirl, short-order cook, of anyone who does his job competently. Why am I condemned to despise myself so totally the moment I am not "making" something, braiding letters into words into sentences, tracing webs of lines or patterns of color to transcribe imprints of what has delighted my eye? A matter of destiny? If so, it started in childhood, as a kind of epiphany: the pure delight of sharply realizing the miracle of being alive, of being able to see and to feel, that only real one of all miracles—sheer existence!

I am writing this in the Holland of my birth. Beyond the window stretch the endless fields covered with late snow. They are crisscrossed by frozen canals and, as in a seventeenth-century painting, tiny figures of skaters sail through white meadows under a greenish-grey sky. On the horizon phantoms of trees feather around triangular farm roofs. If I disregard a blotch of buildings going up on my left, this still is the surviving, archetypal landscape of childhood, the eternal empty landscape where nothing pretends, nothing is picturesque. It is a landscape offering nothing to see but the eternally changing confrontation of light with water, land and sky, color and bleakness, stillness and turbulence, luminous transparencies, impenetrable opacities.

I always must return to draw or paint this emptiness bursting with mood. It has remained mine, although I know how through the years, imperceptibly, I have become an American—have bartered American idiosyncrasies, totems, and taboos for my Dutch ones—this landscape remains mine. To it I can go home again. Now, surrounded by it, I smoothly switch back to childhood.

I remember a warm, late spring day. I was perhaps five years old. Mother had taken us to a little garden café on the edge of town. On a bandstand under trees, a trio was playing sentimental light classics. I remember them photographically: the balding violinist in his pince-nez, doing his vibratos, the large-breasted blond lady, playing the grand with velvety little hands, the young cellist with his beautiful frown.

As my brother was playing with other children in the sandpit, I managed to escape across a wooden bridge over the brook and lie down in the high grass. Daisies, clovers, and a hairy purple flower were on the level of my eyes, so close that they were huge, out of focus. A big brown bee landed on the purple flower and started to suck. I forgot to be afraid of the bee, just watched. Or rather, not I watched, for all at once there was no more I. Through these eyes something was watching itself and a feeling, a state, a condition I have never forgotten, a bliss—aware of being bliss—had replaced what had been me.

The trio was playing a little tune I have never heard again, a long forgotten hit—but which now, half a century later, I can recall at will at any moment. The tune condensed all life, all longing, love-sickness, joy, sadness, death, transfiguration, eternal life, and mystery. The flowers are still there, the trio is still playing, the bee never finished sucking. If only I could tell the long dead composer how his tune sounds through all eternity. I am still drawing grasses when my mind craves quiet. It was the beginning.

I was eleven years old when I was thrown together with an Austrian boy whose hobby it was to pull the wings off living flies, which he was very adept at catching. In horror and powerlessness I watched the tiny creature lying on its back on a newspaper, fumbling with six puny hands and feet, rubbing them together desperately. Herman watched in amused fascination. What I saw I hardly finitely precious, unique, yet in all its limitless variety in constant state of interpenetration, of Oneness, just my wn eccentricity? Am I perhaps *homo religiosus* groping is way by mere chance through the conduit called art?

I could well see myself in a former incarnation painting icons in some cell, peeping through the window at the girls' legs I have so slandered, and switching to painting Madonnas and unicorns in fields resplendent with grasses, wild flowers and small animals. In those days I would not have had to call myself "an artist"; I would have been a simple artisan.

What made one into "the artist" then, was perhaps a betrayal: a painting once seen in a museum that made the ego say, "I can do that too, I can do better! I too shall hang in museums!" The temptations and the delusion to conquer the world "doing your thing," the seduction and hallucination of fame within reach, the high treason to the ecstasy; the sadness beyond words of letting the ego, that little self, take over to exploit the original impulse that came from the depth of being, where the indwelling spirit is. Exploit, I said, not transcribe and glorify. Exploiting makes the glorification into neurotic self-glorification, surrender to the limitless demands of the ego, insatiable in its elbowing for recognition, approval, fame, power, thus leading from betrayal to betrayal.

I know where my work springs from ego, for there it is stimulated by praise and discouraged by neglect. Yet suffering and powerlessness seem to be conditions for the breaking in of the vision that makes all new again.

One joins the art rat race. The rat race is a game in which if you win you surely lose and if you lose you may

dare say. I saw the crucifixion of all creatures. I started to try to draw the mysterious iridescence of insect wings. There were other times when life repeated its urgent invitation to enter it. Blossoms. Candle flames. Christs-in-glory.

Being back in Holland, where the eye is so constantly bewitched by shifts in mood and color, by shafts of light through fluid cloud formations, I ask myself, "What makes other people into artists?" It is nonsense to suppose that they all have such extraordinary surplus of creative energy, more than those who become merchants or lawyers. So what is it?

In Holland too, of course, the painters have gone abstract and joined the succeeding waves of op-, pop-, minimal art. Why do they paint in herds and trends? Painting after all is an activity unthinkable without the eye that perceives, the eye that corrects and controls the canvas from inception to finish, however much one talks about automatism. Have they suddenly developed op-eyes, pop-eyes, minimal-eyes? Or have they torn out the perceiving eye in this Western Europe, where the light gave birth to landscape, still life, seascape painting (no wonder impressionism was born from the vaporous light of Western Europe!)? This delight of light is enough to fill a thousand painters' lives, to inspire endless approaches to painting . . .

Perhaps artists in a small country inevitably feel that they must join, if not spearhead, the fashions that sweep Paris or New York. It is just too unbearable to be regional or provincial in a time of space exploration. Wouldn't a man rather walk blind through the surrounding splendor?

It is one of the minor fallacies and impostures of this century that the main effort, the only hope of artists should be directed at being discovered as absolutely original, sui generis.

It takes a flash of insight to have finished with this delusion and to start the search and struggle for authenticity, wherever that might lead, even if it should be away from one's first love, painting. It led me to drawing what my eye sees. It led me to doctor and to draw in Lambaréné, to write on Albert Schweitzer and on the meaning of drawing. Later it led me to draw Pope John and his council, to discover that I could not say all about the council in drawing and painting and so I wrote again.

Such searching, disguised as versatility, is of course heretical and reprehensible in a time where to be successful, the artist too must be a specialist, restricted to the making of pictures. Preferably he should paint the same picture over and over again, as the trademark which makes critics and dealers crow, "He has found himself!" I am definitely not sui generis. I don't even want to appear "original," for I am aware of being related to and rooted in a dozen traditions; I am all too interchangeable with all other men in the basic conflicts, aspirations, fears, delusions, and enlightenments that lie between birth and burial. This conviction makes it bearable to write this without reserve and restraint.

Whatever makes others into "artists," I discovered that for me art has never really been an end, but at least as much a means. As a tool for self-exploration and clarification of what life is about, I found it a merciless tool, unwittingly chosen, to overcome all delusions about one-

self and the world. A tool to discover w
"work of art," completed or incomplete
ure, becomes the inescapable confronta
what I am, and what I am not. The mos
judges me precisely on the graph between
my death and is, if not the Last, certainly t
ment. The act of drawing is a merciless ai
oneself.

In painting, especially in contemporar
there are a thousand devices to fool yourself
shock or the charm of color, the elegance of
surface, the seductions of style . . . Painting, n
can be derivative, elaborating on art forms alre
covered by others. But drawing with my pen on a
paper—a sumac, a city street, a naked woman—I
my own. A built-in graphologist is always ready to
nose the sureness and the truth as well as the hesita
and pretensions of my line and to point out the sligh
phoniness. The act of drawing happens to be the antid
to phoniness. Even supposing my drawing has passed t
graphological test, does it show a naked female human b
ing or a piece of vulgar eroticism? Hate? Eros? Agape? I
my sumac alive? Does my street pulse? The verdict is
right in front of me. Irrevocably, for I can beautify nothing in my pen drawing. I can only discard.

Do similar childhood revelations, those "peak experiences" that are at the origin of my compulsion to shape in lines and words and color the fleeting world of grasses, faces, land, and sky lie at the origin of other artists' compulsion too? Are they a necessary ingredient of what one calls art? Or are those early intuitions that all that is, is

well win and find the awakening again and again. Although there may never be a repeat performance in the meadow, life will open again where least expected.

At a cocktail party of all places, when a sudden stillness outshouts the chatter, and, suddenly out of all the eyes speaks That. Behind all those eyes, mine included, stands That looking at itself. Inside the carefully chosen clothes the bodies are clearly naked, not obscenely or coldly or clinically naked, but showing life playing its fleeting games in flesh. Its process. For through the splendor of her mating mask, a girl suddenly unveils her baby face, her old wife's face, her skull. Or it may happen when unsuspectingly walking along a road, a shudder of wind makes a whole planting of young poplars dance . . . when in a plane as the abrupt change of pitch of the engines should send you into panic, you feel yourself smile . . . when in a subway suddenly you look out of all those eyes at the thing sitting on your seat . . . It cannot be coaxed, It invites Itself. Should I try to force It with a drug, it would be I who did the inviting and what invites the "grace of God" is not I. I can only chase it away. It is from this "grace of God" that one's vision and hence one's work always starts all over again, that resurrection follows the death and despair of each day.

In drawing I find the tranquilizer for the ego's madness. It seems to be an activity springing from my quiet central self, a center of awareness, which remains after peeling off the layers of delusion. No wonder a drawing can only speak privately, softly to another self, not to the social phantom of the other, neither to multitudes as fashionable paintings always appear to do! But then, is it my function to pseudo-communicate with a mob? I am not Hearst or Beaverbrook!

Choice, says a Zen sage, is the sickness of the mind. This sounds like sheer inanity to the Westerner for whom "free choice" is an article of faith. The vision in the meadow, in the subway, seems to indicate that although choice is indeed available to the artist, it is at the same time fatal. His is the choice of a sparrow to sing like a nightingale. That wonderful painter Boudin knew it: "I am just a little lark, I sing my simple song to the gray clouds."

Pestered and pursued by the original vision, suddenly the whole phenomenon called art world reveals itself as the empty figment, the trivial, frivolous game, played with credulous artists as pawns by the Courreges, the Diors, the Pierre Cardins of the art marketplace and their hangers-on . . .

Does this "art world" at least produce art? Oh, why join the philistines in the eternal quarrel about what precisely is art! Since it all is displayed in the museums and sold in the shops called galleries, let us by all means grant it the coveted description "art"!

Yet all too rarely it is an art of and for the whole man, in which the senses as well as the spirit find delight and fulfillment (instead of entertainment, *Kleinkunst*), an art that disdains being "exciting," and that at any rate aspires to being high art. In the confusion of all values in which we live it is probably too much to ask for high art. The sculptor Manzu, about whom I recently wrote an article (NCR), a Henry Moore, sometimes Picasso or Marini, still clearly aspire to it; I cannot think of many other well-known names.

I shall try to indicate what I call high art. In music, Mozart and Bach are still the ones to exemplify this: art that gives us hope about the human condition. Has it not happened to you, that when in black despair you turned on your radio, resigned to listen again to the day's atrocities between the inane commercials and the noise of non-music, that suddenly, unexpectedly, a Mozart aria filled your room and the tears sprang into your eyes: there is hope! Man is *not* garbage, he has produced this miracle out of his living substance! Man is *not* the lowest form of life; there is hope!

In painting and drawing, Rembrandt is the supreme example. A tiny drawing of a landscape near Amsterdam compresses the eternity, the fragility, the transiency and tenderness of the organism that is the world. In the portrait of a man there is a particular face, very much that of Jan Six or of Titus, and at the same time these are the features of what is centrally human. Behind Jan Six and Titus then, I discern the features of the central man, of Christ. Sign and triumph of hope, of that ever-possible resurrection in which man's dignity precisely consists.

Look at a nude woman by Rembrandt and you see how his compassion shows that, what has but started to flower a moment ago, is already so very close to its final fading. Rembrandt seems to paint what I had seen in meadow and dying fly, and lost because of the betrayal by the ego.

One day I stood in the grotto of Lascaux, looking at the primeval bulls, drawn on rock thirty thousand years ago by the men of Aurignac. These artists had, long before the dawn of history, been handling a language which we all can still clearly understand. They had drawn their sacred animals in a flash only possible after endless observation. Suddenly the animal must have started to live within that cave-dweller artist, my direct ancestor, and revealed itself, so that in one great sweep he could note it down on the rock—both the animal and his own moment of insight. He and I find our insight by seeing. There may be many ways to liberation and insight, this one happens to be his and mine!

Drawing is a way of seeing that becomes a way toward life, even a way of life, in which I become one with my fellow creatures, with landscape, with city, sun and rain. Drawing thus becomes a religious discipline, a probing of truth, a perception of Reality, a meditation by eye and hand combined. In the act of drawing the whole person is involved. The eye perceives, intellect and feeling are taut; a reflex flashes from eye to hand, going through the whole body and somehow through all that is called mind and heart. All the hand does, is to precipitate a line, provided it obeys perfectly and is not interfered with by the meddling, cheating ego. All progress in drawing comes from the training of the reflex arc and the short-circuiting of the self-conscious "personality." The hand has to become the unquestioning seismograph that notes down something the meaning of which it knows not. True drawing is always "original" in this sense, but it is only perceptible to the aware observer.

When Manzu speaks of his utter paralysis during the modeling of Pope John's portrait, he really speaks about the invasion of the ego into the process of modeling that is much like drawing. The thought "Here am I, Manzu, modeling the Pope!" is enough to produce catatonic panic. I have not only gone through these moments of complete paralysis drawing a Schweitzer, a Graham Greene or a Toynbee, but even while drawing a gorilla in the zoo: "Here am I, Franck, drawing my first gorilla." Finished! It happens the instant, unable to become what I draw whether Toynbee or gorilla, I pit myself against it. That moment the sweat of angst starts dripping into the eyes of an impotent wretch.

During the act of drawing, a sleeping pauper, Albert Schweitzer, a dead seagull, a cardinal, and a cabbage become equivalent: beings. And I am not more than the hand that notes them down. Entering into the stream of living, unique forms, my hand moves with the fleetingness of life on the wing, catching nothing, merely tracing a line. During the act, having become a pauper, seagull, cardinal, I know these beings from the inside out. The eye is steady, it allows all to pass before it, accepting it impartially. But make no mistake, before the seismographic impulse of the reflex arc that starts in the eye reaches the hand, it has traveled through the existential whole of the person who draws and hence it shows what he sees and what he is, without compromise.

While drawing Vatican II, I became more involved, identified with it, than I had bargained for or dreamed possible. I am no hero-worshiper—beings are equivalent —yet while drawing the Pope John of his last years, I saw neither hero nor saint, but the incarnation of the Holy Spirit in our time. With Pope John the church seemed on the brink of celebrating the liberty and dignity of each human being, because it saw the Christ at his core, as man's limitless potentiality, his always available convertibility to what he really is. Thus it would redeem and respiritualize our agonizing world of hatred, greed, ignorance, and murderous violence. Pope John, as I saw him while drawing, had become this vision. In him I saw all conflicts reconciled, all divisions healed. *Aggiornamento* was to be neither breast-beating nor streamlining, but nothing less than new awareness. Metanoia.

The death of the great prophet and the withering of his council, brought me, who am not even a card-carrying Catholic, to the edge of deep melancholy. I still found his message alive, but only in the periphery of the church, while the institution seemed to lack the vision, the immense vitality John had emanated up to his last breath. To get that council out of my system, I wrote three books. It was not enough. Displaced, satiated with the drawing of scarlet cardinals, patriarchs, and Rome baroque, I returned to Warwick, N.Y., unable to banish the hope Angelo Roncalli had awakened.

On the banks of the creek opposite my house stood the ancient dry-masonry foundation of an eighteenth-century water mill used as a garbage dump, grown over with weeds. I cleaned it out, restored it, and built a huge roof over it that in its form symbolized the flight of the Dove. It became a chapel to honor Pope John. I called it "Pacem in Terris." I built with one helper. I did all sculptures, stained glass, and mosaics of the symbols of the great religions myself, for I wanted it to be one man's witness.

I forgot about critics and dismissed the fear of being thought a crank and let the vision realize itself. I saw Pacem in Terris as an experiment in communication, transdenominational but not syncretistic. I hoped in the face of the fashion and the menace of the Absurd to make something to deny the Absurd. On its facade I placed as a motto:

> I built Pacem in Terris (Peace on Earth) a place of inwardness, in honor of Angelo Roncalli, John XXIII, Prophet of human solidarity. Following him I built on ancient foundations, anchored in rock, vivified by living water.
>
> May the Spirit soar and make us creatures realize our unity.

Now, on weekends all summer long, it is open to all. And they come and come back, mostly young people, Catholics, Protestants, Jews, blacks, whites. It means something to them. Hope? They play their guitars; they sit, think, talk. There have been spontaneous eucharistic celebrations, a Protestant and a Catholic Worker wedding, readings, concerts. A concert, in September 1968, united a dozen Franciscan novices in their habits, a black gospel singer, a Jewish cantor, a Hindu sitarist. Some 120 people came to listen and were offered bread and wine on the edge of the creek, without comment.

Shooting out of the earth in front of the chapel stands the huge hand of Christ I built from old beams. On its fingers are carved the names tainted by the cruelest crimes against men in our time: Guernica, Lidice, Auschwitz, Hiroshima, South Africa, Selma, Budapest . . . ever more.

Recently a letter followed me from Iowa to Holland. A college freshman, a girl I never met, wrote:

> I soon began to discover an entire new world surrounding and involving me as a result of my experiences with Pacem in Terris. I cannot begin to express what these feelings and ideas are, but I know Pacem in Terris is now a part of me. . . . I have found so much about life and myself through Pacem in Terris. . . . Perhaps I will even be able to help someone to find what I found there.

But many of the young people I do meet all summer long. Others write their comments on a writing pad that always lies in Pacem in Terris. Through these meetings and these comments I have met a young America that in its profound humanity does not conform to the stereotypes we have professed about ourselves for so long and have made others believe about us. After so many years, through Pacem in Terris, at last I became rooted in the American soil and reality. If the chapel gives these young people hope, they returned it to me a thousandfold. Where Babbitt is dying, Christ may well be rising!

Glenn T. Seaborg is director of the Atomic Energy Commission. He was appointed to his present position by President John F. Kennedy in 1961 and was reappointed by Presidents Johnson and Nixon.

Mr. Seaborg is considered one of America's most distinguished scientists. A Nobel prize winner in chemistry, he is noted for the discovery of several elements which are basic to the research in the development and uses of nuclear energy. Before assuming the leadership of the Atomic Energy Commission, Mr. Seaborg was chancellor of the University of California at Berkeley.

4

Glenn T. Seaborg

The Pain of Having Unused Answers

There is no doubt that the impressive age in which we live, filled with its spectacular scientific and technical achievements, its material growth and rapid pace of change, is also an age of great turmoil and anxiety. And we do not have to examine conditions very deeply to see why our progress is paralleled by new problems, or in some cases is the source of those problems.

For one thing, change has always been unsettling to human beings and today we are experiencing a rate and scope of change men have never known. Another cause of our current unrest stems both directly and indirectly from the new knowledge and power that science and technology have given us. Such knowledge and power impose tremendous new responsibilities on man. And they are responsibilities from which we cannot turn because they involve his deepest relationships with nature, his man-made environment and his fellowman.

These relationships, growing tighter and more complex each day, are even more a source of concern and responsibility to scientists, who have to a great extent made the world what it is today and who also are a source of much of the knowledge and power that will determine its future. But, as I hope to point out later, there is much anguish in our inability to apply all the know-how and resources we have as fully and as quickly as our problems demand. And admittedly we still have much to learn in many areas.

As I have often stated before—and this seems to be more evident each day—science and technology are bringing us face to face with our morality. They are forcing us to do more than pay lip service to those things we have said we believed in—such things as the brotherhood of man, the dignity of the individual, greater social justice, an understanding and respect for nature, and a reverence for all life. All these beliefs have taken on a new and vital significance as a result of developments in our scientific age. We now see that our very survival is at stake if we do not use our newfound knowledge and power to translate more of our ideals into realities.

Another source of our unrest and anxiety today lies in our trying to fulfill rising expectations, particularly in trying to organize and apply our resources and talents to meet these ends. This is a source of personal frustration for me. As a scientist and government administrator, I am painfully aware of the disparities that exist in the world, *but I am even more disturbed by the knowledge of the world as it is as contrasted with the vision of the world as it could be.*

To some extent, the source of my frustration is the diverse material that routinely crosses my desk in Washington. On one hand there are the newspapers, magazines, reports, and other current sources of information which portray in harsh and often negative terms the state of the union and the world. At the same time come the scientific papers, the journals, the speeches, letters and words of scientific and government colleagues which show many of the important accomplishments of the times as well as pointing to the enormous potential for the future.

Here are *two different worlds*—or outlooks on the world. I feel caught between them, knowing there is truth on both sides, that not every proposition is an either-or one, that not every situation is black or white, and that there is a gamut of possibilities for the future, but also convinced that we are treated today to too much negativism and self-defeating despair.

Yet on the basis of all that I learn in Washington, in our national laboratories, our universities, and my trips across the country and around the world, I see reasons for being optimistic about the future. I see enormous possibilities for good—for world development, for wider social and economic gain combined with a better distribution of this gain, for a fuller, healthier, and more creative life for more of the world's people. And I see the possibility of much of this through the growth and wise application of science and technology *if* only we could somehow find the ways to do so.

Over what points do I feel the deepest frustrations?

How could we use our science and technology creatively to accomplish those goals which appear today to be almost a necessity for the human race? And what are some of the problems we would have to overcome to do this?

Perhaps the most basic problem the world faces today—as it is relevant to almost all our other problems—is that of population control. I will not comment on the moral controversy involved in this problem other than to point out that since—through our medical advances—we have fostered and universally accepted as moral and natural our increased longevity and the reduction of infant mortality that is in effect a form of "death control," it would seem unnatural and immoral not to accept and foster "birth control" on the same basis. This, of course, is the view of a scientist who believes that there is as an inescapable logic to morality as there is to science. And perhaps this typifies all my frustrations—as I'm sure it does most scientists—that we as a society are so shortsighted—and act so slowly to conditions like the population explosion which we know will lead us into a dilemma.

One thing we are beginning to realize is that perhaps the key to the population problem is not solely the dissemination of information and birth-control methods but includes the convincing of millions that their security and well-being are no longer dependent on having a large number of children, and that fewer children could mean a better life for themselves and those children. In fact, it may be a lack of man's own knowledge of his ability to survive today that is his greatest threat to survival.

Paralleling the efforts toward population control are those to increase food production around the world and thus stave off the massive famine that some have predicted for the years ahead. Here again it is painful to me to see so many people resigning themselves to the idea that certain areas of the world face mass famine in the years ahead regardless of what can be done. And particularly since there has been some encouragement lately in agricultural developments.

At the moment the most encouraging signs are the results of the record crops that have been produced in several Asian countries where new high-yield plants, of such staple foods as wheat and rice, have been introduced. The success of these crops after their introduction, the increasing acceptance of them by the farming population, and new developments being worked on by plant scientists, are all leading some agriculturists to talk of a "Green Revolution" that could help turn the tide against hunger.

There is also work being done toward the agricultural development of presently unproductive land. In my own agency, the Atomic Energy Commission, we are presently conducting long-term studies on the development of large nuclear-powered agro-industrial centers that may someday bring the necessary power, fresh water, and fertilizer to the world's coastal deserts to make these barren and unproductive areas of the world food-producing centers. And we have only begun to tap the vast food resources of the world's oceans. Serving on the National Council on Marine Resources and Engineering Development has made me more aware of the vast amount that can be accomplished in understanding and use of the seas. But this is only part of the food story. The great need for more protein in the diet of many people around the world has been recognized. The development of fish protein concentrate, of high-protein soft drinks now being marketed on a trial basis in some foreign countries, and of biosynthetic protein foods and food additives, are all promising.

The population-food balance is only one of the problems that face man which he *can* solve through the creative use of science and technology. We are, of course, learning that there are other relationships in our environment that we must more carefully balance. We have gone through many decades now of growth and growing productivity with almost utter disregard of the fact that in addition to being greater consumers we are greater wastemakers. In fact, the term consumer is misleading. We are more accurately "users," and most of what we use is eventually returned to nature. Unfortunately, we are today returning too many things too rapidly or in an unacceptable form. As a result, nature is rebelling and we are seeing that rebellion in the form of our polluted rivers and atmosphere and the waste and junk which litter much of our land. Our unplanned growth and productivity are also creating the unacceptable elimination of natural beauty and wildlife, producing eyesores, intolerable noise, and other assaults on our senses.

But all this is not inevitable, or an irreversible process of self-destruction, as some people would have us believe. And this is another source of my frustration—the preponderance of information being offered on the dire consequences of our environmental problems without sufficient emphasis being placed on the ways we can solve these problems. There are ways—and they must be better understood, further developed, supported, and applied as fully and quickly as possible.

This is a case where we must use our science and technology positively and constructively, to gain a fuller understanding of our environment and to halt and reverse the harmful trends associated with our growth and productivity. Important economic and social adjustments will be necessary to do this. The public must be educated to new environmental "facts of life." They will, no doubt, have to learn that there is an economic cost associated with a clean and livable environment. They may have to adjust to new products and new methods of handling waste. We will certainly need public understanding and cooperation in our environmental planning for the future, and in this area new communications techniques will again play an important role.

The efforts toward the development of electric and steam-driven automobiles have been well publicized. Probably less well known are the improvements in industrial filters, the design and construction of more efficient and cleaner incineration plants, efforts to improve sewage treatment systems, and new landfill arrangements for burying solid waste which might otherwise be dumped into our waterways. We could make greater progress in the future, particularly, as I said, if strong public understanding and support of such projects could be established.

Looking farther into the future I can see the day when we may be able, through new advances in science and technology, to productively and economically recycle a good part of the waste we do not reclaim today. The re-cycling of much of our solid waste back into useful natural resources presents one of the most interesting challenges we face. For many scarce substances this will eventually become a necessity even though we may simultaneously develop new and better ways to extract more of them from nature.

Eventually re-cycle should become a way of life—particularly when we have developed nuclear power to the point where it can provide enormous amounts of energy at very low costs. Both extremely cheap energy and a highly sophisticated level of chemical processing are essential to that "way of life"—one in which almost everything we use will be made so that it could easily and economically be reclaimed, reprocessed, and remanufactured into new products. This should give us something approaching "a Junkless Society."

What other areas of great concern are there today which we could alleviate with the help of wisely applied science and technology? Our "urban problem," actually composed of so many related factors—housing, transportation, employment, education, to name a few—is certainly a problem that demands a scientific approach and technological as well as social innovation.

Not to downgrade the enormity of the challenge which faces us in this area—the amount of resources, the time and effort it will take—it is encouraging to see and hear the new thinking on urban development. But here also is an area of great frustration because we cannot even use the means currently at our disposal to alleviate some of our problems, due to our inability to deal as effectively with *people* as we can with *technologies.* And real progress seems to many to be impossible as we are caught between the forces of the various conflicting human factions of our urban society. This aspect of the urban-explosion problem perhaps typifies the moral dilemma that science and technology forces us to face today —that of reconciling the freedom of action of the individual or minority interests (social or commercial) with the demands of rational planning for the ultimate survival of all.

Are there signs of hope that we are at last coming to grips realistically with this problem? For the most part we have recognized the danger of unplanned growth. The "systems approach," used in large-scale scientific and technical missions, such as our space program, is being suggested for most of our new city and community building. New building materials and construction methods are being accepted. In many areas building codes are being revised and labor covenants changed to allow for the use of these materials and methods and to update rigid and often archaic construction practices. The concept of the New City and the Experimental City is being pursued —and should be encouraged. And much is being done, and *much more can be done,* to rehabilitate and revitalize the decaying sections of our existing cities.

It has now been established that during the next decade—the 1970's—we will have to build in this country more than 27 million housing units to accommodate our increasing population and to replace old, decaying dwellings. And it is estimated that such an undertaking will require a total investment of over 650 billion dollars.

If we are to aim for such a goal, and even approach achieving it, we will have to apply a tremendous amount of scientific and technological resources to do the job efficiently and effectively. We cannot build the New America in the style of, or with the methods of, the old. Our new communities must, in addition to livable housing for families of all incomes, have well-planned, efficient transportation systems, utilities systems that supply an abundance of pure water and clean, reliable power, easily accessible educational and recreational facilities and, of course, opportunities for employment.

Obviously, all this is an enormous goal. Some people see this and all the other problems I have touched on as insurmountable tasks. Lately many of them, who have focused more on the problems than on the possible solutions, have given way to despair. This is unfortunate, even frightening, because each one of the challenges ahead of us is, in fact, a race against time. We cannot afford to indulge in any lengthy periods of self-pity, or to spend too much of our time and energy in such exercises as the many historical analyses we have seen recently, comparing our current problems with those that caused the decline and fall of the Roman Empire. There are a few differences between twentieth-century America and ancient Rome, and I believe those differences will have some significance as to our future.

Rather than historical analysis, what we are going to have to do is resort to harsh, realistic, and pragmatic analysis of our current situation—and even here our introspection must quickly give way to decision and action. We are going to have to greatly speed up our information-gathering, our communicating with and understanding of each other, our planning and decision-making, the setting of our goals and the establishing of our priorities.

In conclusion, let me return to the theme of the frustration which I feel, and which I know so many of my colleagues in science and government share, *as we see our people and institutions failing to make the fullest and most beneficial use of all the knowledge and resources this incredible age has to offer.*

One reason for this frustration—and here I think we scientists may be able to change it to a positive, creative force—is our continuing failure to communicate the *human potential* of science and technology to a *large segment* of our population. I stress the "human potential" because, if science is suffering from anything these days, it is the unwarranted criticism that its major projects are overlooking vast social needs or that technology has a dehumanizing effect. Neither of these charges is wholly true, but scientists and engineers must, if they are to gain full public support, make a better public case—a more understandable one—for the human and social benefits that can result from their disciplines and, more broadly, from all science and technology.

In stressing failure to communicate to a "large segment" of the population I am thinking primarily of two groups. The first is composed of those younger people who have somehow turned their back on science because they have been misled into believing or have themselves decided that science and the humanities occupy different and contrary worlds. The second group is the older people—those over thirty—who believe any understanding of today's science is beyond their comprehension.

We must convince the first group that science is a human and, in a sense humanistic, endeavor, one absolutely necessary to the cause—*their cause*—of making the world a place where all people will eventually be able to live well, in harmony with nature and each other, and to enjoy a freer, more creative existence.

To achieve the understanding and support of the second group we scientists must become better public communicators willing to take the time and make the effort to explain our work, its immediate and long-range significance, and its potentially beneficial effect on their lives. And we have to do this on a continuing basis—not just when we need the taxpayers' money to support our own research efforts.

Charles Davis was formerly editor of the *Clergy Review,* taught theology at Heythrop College, served as an expert consultant at Vatican II, and was the author of a number of books on the renewal of Catholic theology. In December 1966, he announced his decision to leave the Roman Catholic Church and to marry a former student, Florence Henderson—a decision that stunned the English-speaking Catholic world.

He explained the theological reasons for his decision in a much-discussed book, *A Question of Conscience*. In this essay he describes the cost of the decision in more personal terms.

5

Charles Davis

My Radical Decision of Conscience

It now seems long ago, but when I bring my memories to mind again the most painful period was the time between my decision and its announcement. Once I had stepped before the public, the tension this required and the subsequent pressure of events carried me along. At that stage it was as if I were taking the part of someone else. I was like an actor. There was a distinction between me and the Charles Davis who was now public property. Inner numbness or perhaps detachment and withdrawal rather than suffering marked the time of publicity. Looking back on it now from a distance I hardly know how I managed to go through with it. The tension that supported me then has now gone, and the memories I have retained of the interviews in which I told various people of my decision possess an acuteness that curls me up inside and makes me realize how much the effort cost me. But at the time some safety mechanism dulled the impact, so that I went forward without a disabling agony.

When the publicity lessened, I was able to turn to my relationship with Florence and enjoy our courtship. Marriage soon followed, and we began to build a new life together. I will speak later of the suffering our decision still brought us in the midst of happiness. But there was no inner turmoil. I have experienced no struggle with qualms of conscience. This is not because I live ironclad in certitude. Such certitude belongs to my past, not to my present existence.

As Christians today we live in convulsive times when many old certainties have been upset. We all have to learn to cope with uncertainty. For me those Christians who remain within the present churches are in an anomalous position, because there is no stable normality in the midst of upheaval. But for the same reason I recognize my own position as equally irregular. We are moving toward a new order for the Christian community. Meanwhile, much is uncertain and no one should make his own position absolute.

At the same time, my many uncertainties are not trouble of conscience about what I have done. The contrast between the values I have experienced since I left and my past state is such as to make a return unthinkable. I remember saying to myself while I was still in the Roman Church that were I not already a Catholic I could not conceive of my becoming one. Well, I am now experiencing that inconceivability from outside. Some people, even when their decision is right and sincere, suffer constantly from the thought that they might have done the wrong thing. Even if it marks me as arrogant and opinionated, I cannot claim that kind of suffering as my own.

I return, then, to the period between my personal decision and its announcement as the time when I had some experience of the cost of a decision of conscience. What stands out in my memory is my sense of loneliness. I formulated my decision to myself on December 4, 1966. Immediately I went to the chapel to lay it before God. I knew the tranquility of resolved conflict, but humanly speaking I felt severed from everyone. During the ten days I allowed for my decision to set firm—or perhaps dissolve—before writing to Cardinal John Heenan, I returned late one night to Heythrop. The quietness shrouding the place was a symbol for me that I was alone, no longer part of the community, cut off from my colleagues and friends. I attended a conference during the same period and felt inwardly isolated, although I knew most of those present well. I could reasonably anticipate sympathy, if not support, from many, but no one could be with me in the inner center where I made my decision. There I had to be alone.

No, not even Florence could be there. From the beginning I foresaw her agreement. I was reassured by it before finally committing myself in writing to the cardinal. But she was not with me in the making of the decision. Nor did I think she could be. Some decisions can be made jointly, but surely not a radical decision of conscience. I had to make my decision and she had to make hers, because in our decisions we were each defining our individual existence as persons before God. Our union together followed, it could not precede our individual decisions.

My own subsequent happiness has been so great and it followed so quickly upon my decision that I should be embarrassed at any attempt to present me as exemplifying the suffering involved in making a decision of conscience. Moreover, whatever the reasons—and I would not myself discount a natural psychological explanation—I felt more than my usual strength during the crisis. I am therefore most disinclined to dramatize what I did. At the same time, reflecting upon my experience, I think I can to some extent discern the nature of the suffering inherent in decisions of conscience when these cut deep.

A radical decision implies risking oneself as a person, and the suffering involved is loneliness. This suffering is creative, because it is the necessary condition for making a truly personal contribution to the human community. What is at stake in a fundamental decision is one's identity and existence as a person. In more superficial decisions one is not wholly committed. If in such instances a decision should be mistaken, it can be changed again without redefining one's personal identity or essentially altering one's relations with other people. Even decisions of conscience may be quite limited. They may be merely a question of making moral choices within the context of the same style of life. A fundamental decision affects the defining characteristics of the person and consequently determines the very nature of his relations with others. It is a total commitment because the whole self is involved in its effects. If the decision should prove wrong, it can be rectified only by again becoming a different person for oneself and for others. The key decisions of conscience, such as faith or unfaith, this faith or that, are of this kind.

The temptation is to avoid any fundamental decision, particularly when this would involve a break with the stance in life which one has inherited and into which one has been socialized. It is easier to go along with others without disturbance in the same mode of life with the same beliefs in the same community and network of relations in which one has been brought up. Many in that way remain where they are because they are unwilling to decide for themselves. Others change, but by drifting with the tide—not by a personal decision. Change as well as resistance to change can be the avoidance of a truly personal commitment. In both cases there is a fear and a refusal to risk one's personal identity and existence in a decision that affects and redefines one's inmost personality. Instead, one's inner personal core is protected by being enclosed in a role received from outside, to which one remains fundamentally uncommitted. But such protection is death, because here he who saves his life will lose it and he who loses his life will save it.

To make a fundamental decision is necessary to experience loneliness. Here I would distinguish inner loneliness from external isolation. The extent to which someone who steps out of line finds himself isolated varies considerably. Sometimes he will find little or no support during his life. Even if he is right, his stand may not be vindicated until after his death. Many who prepared the present renewal in the church did not live to see it. At other times, agreement and support may be immediately forthcoming. But in either case the inner loneliness is inescapable. If the decision is truly personal, it is made alone. It will never be the mere reflection of existing attitudes, and support for its personal contribution must follow and cannot precede the decision itself. Moreover, the person can never invoke the support as a substitute for the responsibility he himself bears for the decision.

This is so even when the decision is taken within the context of the Christian community and tradition. The relation between community and the individual is always dialectical, that is, it consists in mutual interaction. The individual is formed by the community and becomes a person only in and through the community. But the community exists and is sustained only by the actions and decisions of its individual members. What they do creates the community. If they refuse the creative contribution of their individual decisions, the community and its tradition will drift into decadence. It is by the truly personal decisions of its members that a community with its tradition is transmitted as a living reality through different generations and cultures.

Paradoxically, the suffering inherent in the lonely responsibility of personal decision is creative inasmuch as it creates community. The Catholic tradition on sexual morality has fallen into stagnant corruption because for too long Catholics were afraid to take the responsibility for truly personal decisions in this matter. But that would have required a deeper reassessment of their position as Christians vis-à-vis the church than they were prepared for.

The call to Christian faith is a demand for a truly personal fundamental decision. This is so clear in the Bible that I am surprised at the manner in which some writers have defended their continued adherence to the Roman Catholic Church. For example, Michael Novak in *Commonweal* (Nov. 1, 1968) writes: "For to be a Catholic is to stand among a historical people. *I cannot escape what I am*" [my italics]. Again, he describes himself as "feeling somehow both blessed and cursed in finding myself a Catholic, both blessed and cursed in finding myself an American." This is to make one's position as a Christian a function of natural inheritance and the Christian community a natural community as distinct from a voluntary community to which one belongs by a personal decision. The Christian church is indeed a historical people, but not one to which one belongs by birth.

The history of salvation is usually seen as beginning with Abraham's decision to leave his natural community at the call of God. He left his father's house and country, together with his inherited gods, to go into the land God promised to him and his posterity. If a new historical people took its origin in Abraham, it was not enough to be a descendant of Abraham to belong to it. Paul makes that clear in his theology of the chosen people in Romans, chapter 9. And he is only echoing the teaching of the prophets, which was repeated against the Pharisees by John the Baptist. Further, modern historians underline the fact that the unity of Israel as a people was not in fact primarily ethnic. Israel was a selection of tribes from among those of the same stock and came to include much of the indigenous Canaanite population. The unity of Israel was religious, based on a common acceptance of the covenant.

And the Christian church itself took shape as a distinct community because Christian Jews were prepared to separate themselves from their own people when faith in Christ demanded this. They saw themselves indeed as the true Israel, but not on the ground that they could not escape what they were as Jews—an attitude which would have kept them in Judaism. On the contrary, they remembered or attributed to Jesus sayings that repudiated any reliance upon natural inheritance or kinship. People coming from East and West would enter the kingdom before the children of Abraham. A man must hate father and mother to follow him. His word would divide families. And his brother and sister and mother were not his blood relatives who stood waiting for him, but those who did the will of God.

"I cannot escape what I am" is a strange defense for belonging to any Christian church when a church can claim the name Christian only insofar as it represents the new community founded by Christ upon the new covenant, demanding like the old covenant men's free acceptance—a community transcending every natural or inherited boundary. Moreover, it is but an evasion—"bad faith" in Sartre's sense—to disclaim interest in and responsibility for the official corruption of the body to which one belongs. To be a Roman Catholic is to be implicated in the activity of a particular organized church.

Christians today in general are divided in their understanding of the church. I myself do not see the historical people in which—by a free decision—I stand as limited to any of the existing churches. But agreement ought even now to be possible in the truth that to be a Christian is a matter of a personal decision, not a function of inherited background. And since being a Christian means belonging to the Christian community, the chosen relation to that community is at the heart of the radical decision of faith. To demand a fundamental personal decision in relation to the church instead of acquiescence in inherited positions is to expose many Christians to much suffering. But in that suffering lies the only hope of a genuine renewal of the Christian church as a community of believers.

Earlier I spoke of the suffering that still continues long after the crisis of my own decision. Again, though this suffering is not remarkable, it may serve as an indication of the kind of suffering involved in a decision of conscience. It may be described as severance and criticism.

Severance is not the same as loneliness, though the two are intimately related. Loneliness may be offset by sympathy and support from various quarters. Severance is healed only by being reunited to those from whom one has been cut off. A radical decision of conscience will often cut one off from those to whom one is intimately united by blood, by love and affection, by friendship and common enterprise.

I have been fortunate in retaining the love and friendship of most of those to whom I was united in the past. But I cannot pretend that the relationships are the same as before. There are barriers; there are, perhaps unconscious, limits. I see some of those most ready with sympathy falter in moments of doubt and incomprehension, wondering how far they should support. The worst situation is where there is love but blank bewilderment, where the level of communication is not such as to make discussion possible. I would if I could surrender much public sympathy in order to heal the wound of severance with a few.

Severance is a constant ache for anyone who has had to make a radical break with the past. What is worse, I do not see clearly how this suffering is itself creative, either in myself or even less so in others. It is part of the cost of following one's conscience. I see the inevitability of it, but what does it positively contribute? It has to be taken up into the general mystery of suffering and seen by faith as redemptive. But its presence is for me chiefly a sign that our full redemption is still awaited in hope.

Some may be surprised that I place criticism under the heading of suffering. But I have learned by experience not readily to believe those who declare themselves immune to criticism. I once thought myself comparatively indifferent to it. I am not indeed speaking of a friendly but critical discussion of one's opinions. No intellectual could mind that. I am talking of criticism that is intended to hurt personally. My testimony is that it does. It is not the rejection of one's opinions but the rejection of oneself that hurts—the attempt to diminish one as a person. I have received letters from people whose uneducated abuse could not possibly affect me intellectually, but the sheer force of their desire to injure, indeed erase me, has been a sickening experience. Nor is it anything but lowering to read attempts in print to degrade one as a person.

I admit that I personally have been remarkably well treated. But I have received enough blows to guess what might happen to a person who seriously offended common opinion. We are social beings who need an atmosphere of acceptance and love in which to grow and flourish. And so we are vulnerable to criticism that rejects us as persons. If people are to make truly personal decisions, they need, not primarily agreement, but a love that is willing to accept them for what they are. Otherwise they will wither before the blast of the criticism which aims at personal annihilation. And some criticism of that kind they will have to endure in our present state of unfreedom and lack of love.

My predominant experience after my decision has been happiness, not suffering. That may be for some a strong objection against me. Well, even if I shared their view, I could not pretend that my situation is other than it is. All that I can claim in the matter of suffering is that I have caught a glimpse of what might have to be endured in the cause of conscience. With that I ought to thank God he has dealt so gently with me.

Jesuit John L. McKenzie is America's foremost Catholic scripture scholar. His writings include *Authority in the Church* and *Dictionary of the Bible* (winners of the National Catholic Book Award in 1967 and 1966 respectively), and a score of other works. He was president of the Catholic Biblical Association and has received the Cardinal Spellman Award for distinguished contributions to theology by the Catholic Theological Society of America.

His book *Authority in the Church* has brought him trouble as well as awards. He was accused of heresy by Archbishop Robert E. Lucey of San Antonio, and recently it was learned that the book is under scrutiny by the Doctrinal Congregation.

Father McKenzie is professor of Old Testament studies at the University of Notre Dame.

6

John L. McKenzie, S.J.

The Suffering of Staying In

I have been requested to write an essay on the suffering of those who remain within the church in the hope of achieving some good which they do not believe is possible if they depart. I do not consider myself an expert on this or any other type of suffering, because I have been blessed with a life unusually free of suffering. I have enjoyed most of what I have been doing. As far as suffering goes, I think in most instances I gave as good as I got. The few occasions on which I failed to reciprocate are still a bit distressing, but one learns with experience that one sometimes inflicts more pain than one observed at the time.

I have, however, more experience than I desire of persons who have suffered because they have remained within the structure. Some of these incidents are public knowledge and open to public comment; it will be difficult to add to the comments already made, but the topic deserves the effort. Other incidents which I know better are known in confidence, which must be respected.

"Working through channels for change within the structure," "remaining within the structure to reform it," and similar clichés are hollow jokes among those who believe that the church can be saved and is worth saving. One element of their suffering is the uncertainty of their own motivation. What do they really expect to accomplish? Are they even preserving their integrity? Charles Davis will tell them politely that this is just what they are failing to preserve, and James Kavanaugh will tell them less politely.

Are they really hypocrites, pretending to a courage they lack, never pushing their words or their actions to a point which would lead to an open breach with the establishment? Do they remain because they are unable to change their habits, to acquire new skills, to embark on a new life? To embark on a new life is normal at twenty; it is frightening at fifty. Should those of us who are fifty and over therefore disqualify ourselves from participation in discussion on the ground that we are really too cowardly to carry the discussion to its ultimate issue?

On the other hand, their motives are suspect within the structure. If they intend to remain within the structure and work within it, why are they unwilling to work within it in the traditional way, the only way which the managers of the structure understand? Why do they not leave with the other malcontents and allow the church to do its business? You can always tell these crypto-heretics because they seem unable to speak of the church as if they owned it or had founded it.

Few of us are able to answer those who ask, "Why don't you leave the church if you don't like it?" with the equally apt question, "Why don't you leave it?" I am one of the few. But when one's motives are frankly questioned from right and from left, from above and below, it takes more than usual balance of character and clarity of judgment to remain even vaguely sure of one's motives. I do not know whether this should be called suffering.

One at times envies the serenity of Davis and Kavanaugh; one at times envies the serenity of Cardinals James McIntyre and John Krol. One is not sure that on either side the external serenity is surely a token of internal serenity, but let us not question the honesty of anyone. I can understand the serenity of Davis and Kavanaugh; at least they have the serenity of freedom from types like McIntyre and Krol. The price of the serenity of McIntyre and Krol is being like McIntyre and Krol, and I would rather be boiled in oil. It is disturbing to be so far out of sympathy with upper-echelon managers of the organization within which one has chosen to remain. I am encouraged because I know that they, like me, do not own the church, did not found it, and do not really represent it.

Critics like Davis and Kavanaugh have said simply that the church is evil, too evil for them to work with. Your fence-sitter is not capable of this degree of self-righteousness. He knows that there is no human organization in which he may not be required to cooperate with evil. He will not escape this necessity by leaving the church; he will just find himself cooperating with different evils. Like Davis and Kavanaugh, he once thought the church would be different; unlike them, apparently, he learned that it is not, that a dedicated loyalty to the pa-

pacy and the hierarchy can and does at times involve an obligation to do something wicked. This may be his most anguished uncertainty. The time may come when he cannot evade any longer, when he will have to refuse and give up the standing within the organization which he has taken so much trouble to maintain. How much evil can one tolerate on the plea that one can do nothing effective? Continued passive cooperation or nonresistance ultimately corrupts one.

The processes between Cardinal Patrick O'Boyle and his priests in Washington were revolting to every Christian and civilized principle. I can understand the actions of the cardinal; little he has ever said or done would lead one to count on any other type of conduct from him. But I was puzzled and saddened at the number of men who cooperated with him. There must have been some— one keeps saying, there *must* have been—who said, "I believe and I accept the teaching of *Humanae Vitae;* but if you want my help in throwing priests forty and fifty years old into the street, get another boy." Washington appears to be a place where one may not remain in the structure to reform it. But there are people in Washington who are doing it. How long can they remain in this geographical area of the structure?

We have recently had the report of the participation of Cardinal Richard Cushing in a telephone radio program. The cardinal threatened a priest with removal from teaching, exclusion from the program, and other vague penalties; the cardinal did not prepare this speech. It has to be said of Cushing, however, that he has always, sooner or later, exhibited a basic decency. By this time he has probably apologized with genuine humility. It is good that he has—I make the assumption—because he exhibited the worst qualities of the organization within which Father Ouellette and I have chosen to remain. His heart may be as broad as all outdoors, as the program master said, but his manners were the manners of the barnyard.

Somehow he does not seem to be the authentic bully which one sees in O'Boyle, McIntyre, and Krol. Yet he asks the insolent question, "Who paid for your education?" Speaking for myself I made some contribution to my own education. I put more time and work into it than any other person or agency. In return the sponsoring organization has received a number of years of satisfactory service—at least as satisfactory as the educational opportunities. Cushing seems to have in this instance not only the manners of the barnyard but the ethics of the slave-owner. Because "he" has paid for a priest's education—out of his own earnings, I presume?—he has acquired a robot. I take it that if the robot is a good robot, he may expect to become a bishop.

Ouellette should have responded over the air that if the cardinal thinks he acquired a slave by supporting the seminary, the cardinal should send him the bill, minus services rendered, and throw him out. He did not because he is a good priest, who wants to work with the organization in which he believes. Cushing gave him the treatment which such priests must learn to expect from the owners.

Also recently, we have learned of the inner workings of the Congregation of the Holy Office—and I am not going to use the new name; it might imply that I think there is a new reality. The change of name is about as significant as the new name of HUAC.

We have at least learned why the Holy Office insists

on secrecy. With many others I have criticized the secrecy characteristic of so many church operations. I can no longer criticize the secrecy. The procedures of the Holy Office are so shameful that they should be concealed. The mindless monsignor whom Ivan Illich encountered in the dungeons—is that the correct word?—of Palazzo S. Uffizio seemed even to be ashamed of his name. Surely he need not be, although I can understand his hesitation at being associated with this operation.

More interesting, really, is the question, Who is he? What has he done, anywhere, ever, to qualify him to sit in judgment on an intelligent and sensitive man like Ivan Illich? Has he ever spent five minutes in the pastoral and apostolic ministry, written a book or an article, given a sermon or a lecture, written a song or a play or a novel, or even sung a song? As far as that goes, has he read a book? Oh, no, please God, he is a professional expert on heresy by pontifical appointment. He does not have to know anything, do anything, be anything; he is a judge of those who know, do, and are.

The basic trouble with the Holy Office is that it is not a Catholic operation, and I do not mean to imply that any respectable Protestant church would touch it with a 10-foot pole. One of the basic problems of those who remain in the structure is that they so frequently encounter anti-Catholics in positions of decision; and by anti-Catholics I mean people who do not know much about the Catholic Church, do not really believe in the Catholic Church, and are indifferent or hostile to the mission of the Catholic Church.

I cannot pass from this alluring topic without drawing attention to something which commentators on the Illich affair so far have not noticed, and it may be an outburst of my wild historical imagination. The eighty-five questions submitted to Illich were obviously obscene, and everyone noticed this. What struck me as I read them—and you have to read them all—is that this questionnaire was written to be administered "under the question," to use the decent phrase of the old English law, that is, while the witness is on rack. The Holy Office has preserved a medieval documentary form; and one wonders, do they really?—but no, surely not. If the reader can obtain the questionnaire, I suggest that he see whether he can verify my impression.

For some years now I have been an enthusiastic defender neither of canon law nor of clerical privilege, and it may be a false assumption that the bishop of Cleveland and his chancery staff are enthusiastic. If so, I would recommend to them a careful reading of Canon 119, which demands reverence for clerics of all the faithful (excepting monsignors and bishops, possibly, who are not "faithful" in the sense of the code), and defines "real injury" inflicted on clerics as sacrilege; of Canon 120, No. 1, which states the principle of clerical immunity from civil courts; and of Canon 2343, No. 4, which imposes on those who lay violent hands on clerics an excommunication reserved to "the proper Ordinary." Let the chancellor of Cleveland, presumably a canonist, interpret "proper" here; it could create an interesting canonical problem.

No words can be found to describe the bishop who calls the cops on his own priests while they are celebrating mass in church. I would not be caught dead at the kind of liturgical celebration which was held in Cleveland; but if I were a bishop I think I would feel that this is an affair between priests and bishop, and that we do not need the cops to resolve our differences. I would fear that this might be in opposition to the "spirit" of the law, that mysterious reality to which my superiors have so often appealed when they wanted to enforce a prohibition which is not explicit in the documents.

So far I seem to have produced nothing except a recital of a few of the most sordid incidents of relations between ecclesiastical superiors and their subjects; and it will surely be said that I have chosen the atypical as a base for generalization. Atypical? I have gone back no farther than a few months for this recital, nor have I included every such incident made public or known to me personally within this period. If space were available and those involved would permit publication, this piece could easily be ten times as long without any repetition.

I have simply tried to illustrate the topic, which is the suffering of those who remain within the structure, by concrete examples. Few, perhaps, have experienced such things directly; every Catholic ought to suffer when he reads and hears of such things. Who can be happy when the church, which he now realizes is his by free choice as he never realized it before, commits such offenses against Christianity and common human decency?

Suffering which reflected only personal uncertainty and personal insecurity about the future would hardly be worth space in this book. Incidents like those recalled here betray an insecurity in the leadership of the church itself. How deep this insecurity is, how many it affects, we do not know; and this ignorance is no encouragement. My own acquaintance with bishops, limited as it is, leads me to believe that the bishops whom I have named are not typical of the group as a whole. The same acquaintance shows me that this atypical minority is able to impose its image on the entire American hierarchy. Among those who suffer by remaining in the structure count those bishops who dislike the tactics described as much as I do, but who think they are not free to say so. How free I am to say that I detest them will be made known after this appears—and I promise it will be made known.

Yet the insecurity of leadership means that relations within our structure reflect fear and terror far more than one would expect a Christian structure to permit. It is only fair to the prelates named to say that they do not exhaust the possibilities; the list could be lengthened, but I chose these because their actions have been unusually odious, and in the case of two unusually odious over several years. The odious actions manifest panic, the kind of witless terror that leads people to crush one another in a dash for safety.

What good is served by reopening old wounds, by waving bloody shirts which come from episcopal indiscretion, if not from episcopal malice? Why should we wash our bloody shirts in public, to mix two good old metaphors? Let us say that a public disapproval of these actions and of the ideas and motives behind them will do at least as much for the church as the actions themselves. Public disapproval will probably not end such actions until the disapproval is widely expressed for a long time; the most one can hope for now is that bishops who wish to do such things will try very hard to keep them out of the papers.

Let us get down to the ultimate suffering, which I suggested at the beginning when I said that some remain because they hope to achieve some good which does not appear possible if they withdraw. What good do they accomplish? Everyone needs some assurance that his work is not totally wasted. One hopes that one presents to at least a few a vision of the church which they can cherish, which is not purely eschatological, which can be realized. The imperfect church, *semper reformanda,* can remain imperfect and still look much more like a Christian community than it does now. It is flattering but discouraging to hear, especially from one's younger contemporaries, remarks like these: "McKenzie, you and Hans Küng and Karl Rahner et al. talk a nice line, and you come up with a totally credible church. The trouble is that it does not exist outside your minds. You live in a dream church. The official church has practically disowned you, and you know it. You cannot speak in half the dioceses of the country [a little high, I think], the Apostolic Delegate [Vagnozzi] used to tell people it is a sin to read your writings, and at best they do not mention you. You are not asked or consulted even about your skill, and you have absolutely no influence on church decisions. The official church is still the church, as they claim; they run the church, and they, not you, make it what it is. You have made a nice try, old man, and I will remember you with affection after I leave. Keep in touch, because if you continue what you have been doing you will join me before long."

One does not like to hear that one has poured one's life into a rat hole, even when one is convinced that this is the indefectible rat hole. Does the survival of the church, in which I believe without reservation, mean that the church is always and everywhere the living and active presence of Christ? Can one at times live only in the future? Does it ever happen that one is convinced that there is only one church, but that one cannot legitimately associate oneself with the activities of that church where one lives? When the church falls into the hands of an ecclesiastical Mafia, is one justified in saying that it is at the moment impossible to serve the church? These are not idle questions, nor are they easy questions. I think there is no book answer for them. They must be answered by a responsible personal decision, and in the last analysis there is nothing so painful as recognized personal responsibility. I suppose this is also the most creative form of suffering.

I have hinted rather broadly that those who remain in the structure get most of their suffering from the structure. Yet even as I write this I realize that remarks like those paraphrased above from our younger contemporaries get under my skin more deeply than anything that any pope or bishop could say to me. In such exchanges, as I have said, I expect to give as good as I get; and I have to say that what these gentlemen proclaim simply in virtue of their office is largely meaningless to me. If what they say comes from an authentic person, that is another question.

The loss of our members worries me. I sincerely doubt that anyone can really gain, in the long run, by leaving the church; in the short run, they can and do solve their immediate personal problems. I am unable to be very clear about their prospective loss. I am quite clear about the loss to the church. Nino Lo Bello in his *The Vatican Empire* says that the Vatican recognizes that its strength is greatest in areas where poverty, disease, and ignorance abound. He cites Southern Italy as an example. If our authorities continue to offend the educated and the civilized, they may produce a Catholic Church which is entirely like Southern Italy. A charitable judgment is that this is not the intention.

Yet one knows that the church cannot be permanently weakened, much less destroyed, even by its chief officers. While historical generalizations are risky, I will risk the generalization that not since the sixteenth century has the church had so many men in high office who seem likely to destroy it. I am still sure that they will not. There is hope in the Vatican Council II, still barely implemented. There is hope in the rising generation of bishops, clergy, and laity, who will be heard after enough deaths have occurred. There is hope even though a distressing number of this rising generation have severed themselves from the church or given up. There is hope because there are enough of them ready to suffer through the critical years which lie ahead, and I said suffer.

Willingness to suffer is one thing that the ecclesiastical autocrats cannot withstand; they lack it themselves, and they are completely bewildered by those who have it. A bishop friend once told me of a conversation with an archbishop (unnamed only because I have forgotten it) in which the archbishop said, "If you do that, you will never be promoted." My friend said he came as near contempt with an archbishop as he ever has when he answered, “Your Excellency, that was not what was uppermost in my mind when I was consecrated.” There are enough such to sustain the episcopacy and the priesthood as states of life, too many for the existing establishment to expel or discourage.

Were there none willing to pay the price of personal responsibility, then despair would be the only reasonable position. I ask those who have already concluded that despair is the only reasonable position whether this is entirely fair to those who are willing to suffer by remaining in the church which they have chosen.

Frank J. Sheed, founder of Sheed & Ward, Inc., author and lecturer, is best known for his work as a lay theologian and for his street-corner preaching in London, New York, and Sydney. His *Theology and Sanity* established his reputation as a writer of brilliant clarity. His writings have appeared in countless publications, most recently in *Saturday Review*.

7

Frank J. Sheed

The Tragedy of Contemporary Theology

For the theologian *the* tragedy is that the vast majority of the human race does not know Christ and is starved of food he meant men to have. How tragic one feels it to be depends on the value one attaches to Christ's gifts. Certainly an individual theologian, maltreated by authority, stirs Catholics far more; one feels genuine sympathy. But his maltreatment bears no proportion at all to the continuing fact of a vast majority of the human race living and dying without the bread of life.

The church does not exist solely for the good of its members—a service-station to which they resort when they feel the need of refill or repair. Christ brought it into being because there was work he wanted to do in it and through it, the work especially of bringing to the whole world his gifts—truth, love, union with himself and so with his Father.

For every one of us two questions stand challenging: How well is the work being done by the church as a whole? And how well are we ourselves doing our part of it? Whenever we are at boiling point over the defects of the church's officials—thanking God that we are not like Cardinal This and Archbishop That—the second question is there to cool us down. They are unprofitable servants: How profitable does Christ find us? They are insensitive to the world's miseries: How sensitive are we? What sacrifices does our sensitiveness drive us to make?

Christ commissioned his followers to bring his gifts to the whole world till the end of time. This commission has not been carried out with any spectacular success. Nineteen hundred years after, as Vatican II reminds us, there are two thousand million men who know nothing of Christ. There are many reasons for the failure; one stares us in the face. The first word in Christ's commission was Teach. How is he to be accepted by the millions who have never known him, if his followers present them with a dozen Christs and a hundred discordant teachings? For centuries Christendom has been unable to speak with one voice of the most elementary points of his message. And now in the Catholic Church, unity's last stronghold, we have a crisis of faith among the adults, a vast evaporation of faith among the young, discord among the clergy—with no doctrine or practice of the faith I have not heard denied by a priest.

Teaching does not mean simply repeating accurately what Christ did and said. He did not give the apostles his truth embalmed, to be handed on embalmed from generation to generation till the world should end. It was a living mass of truth to be lived. The truth must grow in men. How?

Primarily it grows by being lived, prayed; obeyed, disobeyed; doubted, found good; rejoiced in, suffered in. A truth thus in operation is seen with a clarity that a truth simply heard or read cannot have: it becomes an organic element in the men who live it. It grows also by the mind's exploration of it. One element in the revelation is compared with another, new interpretations are suggested, and examined (with violence often enough); new situations arise, new civilizations indeed, to which it must be applied, in which it must be lived. Philosophy, psychology, archaeology, the natural sciences are making their own separate exploration of man and his world, shedding light which in its first shedding can seem more like darkness, forcing the Christian to reconsider what he has assumed revelation to be saying.

At the heart of the growing process is the problem of language. What the church comes to see must be uttered, stated in words. Otherwise it cannot be communicated. The realities thus communicated may and should vibrate to the depths of our being, but we cannot communicate solely by sharing vibrations. *Cor ad cor loquitur* indeed, heart speaks to heart, but not only by heartbeats. "I would rather speak five words with my mind, in order to instruct others," says Paul (1 Cor. 14:19), "than ten thousand words in a tongue." ("Speaking in a tongue" was one way of vibrating!)

So statements are necessary, but necessarily inadequate. There must always be mystery. We cannot know God as he knows himself, cannot even know ourselves as he knows us. If human words could contain infinite reality, human minds could not extract it. The ultimate realities are unutterable. Yet God has uttered them. Utterance which brought them to birth in men's minds must operate in their growing.

Words can be light-bearing. But there is a danger in them. Men can grow too much attached to forms of words, seeing them as absolutes. Which they are not. A given word can change its meaning, concepts can grow beyond the word in which they were first written. A phrase apt to one culture might be pointless in another. "Father and Son" embodies a splendid concept, but angels for whom "there is no marrying or giving in marriage" must find some key concept other than generation.

If Paul had gone east instead of west, our theology would have been phrased differently. If Augustine had drawn on Shankara instead of Plato, if Aquinas had "baptized" Lao Tse instead of Aristotle, we should almost certainly have had today's avant-garde bewailing the Asian stranglehold and clamoring for the Greeks. As it is, some theologian yet unborn may marry Christian theology to Asian thought forms, to the horror of his more conservative contemporaries.

The *living* of the revelation is by everybody. The *intellectual exploration* is largely for scholars—theologians especially, drawing on the researches of scripture specialists, linguists, and philologists, comparative religionists, scientists of every sort. New interpretations swarm, in vast quantity and of varying worth. "God's desire to be known by us," as I note in *God and the Human Condition,* "has at all times to cope with the marvelous ingenuity of the questing, discovering, uttering mind of man."

Revelation is not given by God for the delectation of theologians. It is meant to bring light and nourishment to all men. How is all this—the daily experience of Christians, the discoveries and theorizings of the learned in their bewildering multifariousness—to be tested against the original revelation? How is it to be shaped teachably and conveyed to the millions of unspecialized men and women in order that, seeing Christ closer and clearer, they may be enlightened by the truth, nourished by the food, vitalized by the life? Even the greatest scholar cannot know more than a small fraction of it, the plain man can make nothing of it. For the millions it might as well not be there at all.

God, having given the revelation, did not simply leave it to take its chance. It is the function of the church—Christ living on in it—to guard the integrity of the revelation and shape it teachably. With so many minds actively at work, changes are forever being proposed, some good, some bad, some enriching, some damaging. There must be a voice to say Yes or No. Otherwise there is no revelation, only a chaos. Authority is necessary not for itself but for the treasures it guards.

How well has the teaching church, the magisterium, carried out its double function of guarding the treasure and dispensing it? Guarding involves not only *censorship,* watching against adulteration by falsehood, but also *stimulation,* encouraging the forces of life and of growth in it. There is not much doubt that over the centuries the censoring has been done with more zeal than the stimulating. Authority can only too easily cross the line into authoritarianism. The law of charity makes more difficulties for officials than for the rest of us, even in normal times. In panic times—as at the Albigensian thrust and the Reformation earthquake—charity has a tough time. Rigidity, excusable perhaps in the crisis, becomes a habit which survives the crisis to the peril of love, which is at revelation's heart. There is a pleasure in the exercise of authority which only high sanctity can resist. Rigidity can come close to rigor mortis.

Rigidity in the guarding of the treasure has affected its dispensing. Many Catholics have been only taught the formulas, not introduced to the reality, the nourishment, the life, that the formulas exist to protect. Concentration on the formulas is a simplification for teachers who know no theology themselves, and to such the teaching of religion in Catholic schools has too often been entrusted. Nor did most of the sermons one heard do a great deal to vitalize. It is a continuing mystery that a teaching church should seem so little concerned to teach its teachers how to teach.

I have noted that there is no doctrine or practice of the church one has not heard denied by a priest. None of these happy innovators are theologians. But it is from men who certainly are that they have got their feeling that anything goes. The real theologians do not hold this themselves, but lesser men think they do. Why?

This is indeed the hour of the theologian, which means that it is a testing hour, an hour of temptation. Not all have come through unscathed. Self-assurance is a continuous peril. One sort of theologian will see difficulties in some of the church's accepted teachings, will study to find how deeply the church has committed herself and her founder to them, will suggest possible corrections and reformulations. But another sort will settle such questions out of hand, on his own say-so. One gets the impression that the pope is not infallible, the hierarchy is not, but vast numbers of theologians are!

Theologians of the first sort walk warily, i.e., humbly. They are continually conscious that there is no map of the Infinite, that even of the finite there are dimensions beyond the range of their vision. The others, though they know all this in theory, seem not to advert to it. Their confidence in their conclusions leaves no place for past or future decisions of the magisterium, in freedom from which they see all hope. But, after all, Protestants have every conceivable freedom and they are hardly setting the world on fire. Like ourselves, they are speaking to fewer and fewer.

For theologians who ignore the teaching church, what standard is there? "Scripture," they would say. But the number of ways of sidestepping scripture is legion. One gets the feeling that scripture is a weapon, not a building tool. The one standard generally acknowledged is the mind of today's world. And indeed the theologian must study it; there is light to be had from it. But standard it cannot be. Not only will today's mind soon be yesterday's, but at its best it cannot, without God's revelation, know what life is all about—why anything (including mankind) exists, or what follows death.

The theologian is necessary, the magisterium even more so. The problem at this moment is that the magisterium has no way of protecting and channeling revelation which will rebuild the diminished confidence, not only of theologians but of the people of God for whose service both magisterium and theologians exist. Anyone who thinks this problem easy has not understood it.

The effect of all that I have been describing upon Catholics generally is a certain dimming and devitalizing. The only vitality visible seems to go into attacks on "the institutional church" or on doctrines long held. Dimming is the word. God is in a cloud, not only of his own infinity, but of man's diminished interest. Christ is in eclipse; priests discuss whether they should leave the church, with him as its founder. I cannot remember when I last heard a sermon on him. Silence wraps the unnumbered millions of the dead—hell and purgatory tacitly assumed nonexistent; heaven, Christ's mother and the saints, the resurrection of the body, not much referred to, felt as embarrassments, all of them.

The church itself has been turned into a question mark. These last ten years there seems to be no assertion or denial that Catholics in good standing are not free to make, so that one is left wondering what is the point or even the meaning of membership. So great a theologian as Karl Rahner talks of the church's being reduced to a tiny handful. This would mean not only a few million more added to the millions upon millions already lacking the food our Lord meant them to have, in darkness for want of the light. It would mean also a reduction almost to vanishing point of the church's power to relieve their destitution.

In the face of so vast a destitution the theologian passes his life. If theology is no more to him than an intellectual game at which he happens to be skillful, it causes him no suffering. But on one for whom God and man are realities, it must weigh heavily—to the point of anguish even, certainly to the draining of the energies of heart and mind for its relief. There is no way in which energies could be more creatively drained.

Herbert Richardson is professor of theology at St. Michael's College, Toronto. He is the author of *Towards an American Theology,* published by Harper & Row.

8

Herbert Richardson

Varieties of Suffering

My most interesting discovery from reading the preceding essays was that there is such a range of experiences of suffering. And I realized that suffering has lost its religious, or creative, value for many of us because we have been inattentive to this range. We have, rather, identified true religious suffering with a single kind of suffering, namely, physical pain and the mortification of the body.

Isn't this true? For example, my local paper ran an article entitled "Jesuit Boot Camp." In it the voluntary flagellation, the bruising with chains, and the systematic frustration of all natural appetites characteristic of the novitiate were detailed. And, to recall another example, hasn't the traditional lenten sacrifice been a giving up of something that we "especially liked"—as if the act had its value solely because it negated a bodily desire?

But to regard bodily pain as the exemplary kind of religious suffering has not been peculiar to the Catholic tradition. A Protestant theologian argued in a lecture that the use of drugs to alleviate pain in persons dying of cancer is dehumanizing and contrary to Christ, whose suffering on the cross should be exemplary for all men. My wife, who was seated beside me during this lecture, turned and commented to me in an indignant whisper that this theologian, a century ago, would have opposed giving anesthesia to women to alleviate their labor pains! So much for the Protestant side of the story . . .

It is lamented by some today that our failure to see any positive religious value in bodily pain and suffering is evidence that a materialistic and secular attitude toward life is everywhere victorious. One doesn't have to be a traditionalist to feel this way. Go back and read these essays again. Don't you feel, as I did, that the one least assimilable within your religious outlook is Glenn Seaborg's? His centers on a single concern: how to eliminate human suffering from this earth. How can we build better houses, have more food, limit population, discover and use talents more creatively? For Seaborg all suffering seems to be destructive. His goal is to remove it, and, to the extent that religion presupposes and validates such suffering, also remove religion as well.

But why did I feel that Seaborg's essay was so secular, so foreign to the religious outlook? Why did it make me so uneasy? It was, I know, the persistence in me of a surreptitious Jansenism, the feeling that—to paraphrase Lord Acton—all pleasure corrupts and absolute pleasure corrupts absolutely. It was a hangover of the old "crucifixional mentality" that measures the suffering of Christ in terms of pints of blood spilled and pounds of cross carried. Oh, I am willing to admit that these persisting medievalisms are now just antique furniture, in my mind. However, it's one thing to admit to such antiques and another thing to get rid of them.

The real me, the anti-antique me, is 100 percent with Seaborg's "Let's Clean Up the Suffering" campaign. For I know from experience that the suffering he programmatically opposes is utterly destructive of persons. And I know that a man's life is not best dignified by admonishing him to endure hunger, disease, and ignorance, but by struggling to free him from such oppressors. My father, who experienced such difficulties in the flesh, once explained this to me in a story. An old man, it seems, was walking down a road and met a boy who was crying. "Little boy, little boy," he said, "why are you crying?"

"I am crying, kind sir, because of my sins."

Next day, same time, same setting. The man, walking down the road, encounters the same boy, still crying. "Little boy, little boy, why are you crying?"

"I am crying, kind sir, because I am hungry."

"Aha," the man wisely nodded, "I thought it would come to this."

One of the things that modern technology is making possible is the sharper distinction between the "creative" and the "destructive" kinds of suffering alluded to in my father's story. This was movingly stated by Mrs. Martin Luther King Jr., in an essay in *The National Catholic Reporter,* when she said:

> It is essential to distinguish between destructive and creative suffering. The world today is dominated by

> sorrow and agony. The majority of mankind is deprived of the basic essentials for life; it survives and endures under the whip of oppression and hunger. This suffering is negative and life destroying. It cannot be justified or rationalized by any philosophy.

Before we could do something about making the basic essentials of life available to all men, it was impossible to distinguish between the virtues of "weeping for sins" and "weeping for hunger." Life required that men learn to endure deprivation, bodily pain, and ignorance—and this virtue of endurance, no less than the virtue of moral sensitivity, had to be inculcated by the church. But the problem, in this situation, was that the two types of virtue could easily be confused. The sheer endurance of poverty, fasting, and pain could come to displace the development of moral conscience as the primary interest of religious life. This is why technology has created a crisis for Christianity today. It forces the church now to engage full time in the harder task: the development of the human spirit. It forces it to face the harder kind of suffering: the creative suffering that is involved not simply in enduring pain, but in growing into the fullness of spiritual life.

One of the odd things I have discovered when speaking about the suffering involved in the growth of the human spirit is that people sometimes suggest that such an experience is utterly foreign to them. I confess that I even wondered to myself, as I read the essays of Franck and McKenzie, if I would count their experiences as "suffering." Franck's seemed a bit too precious to me; McKenzie's a bit too acrimonious. Then I suddenly prodded myself and wondered, "Hey, Richardson, your job is to be reflecting on the honestly reported experiences of suffering presented by several other people and here you are trotting out some Scholastic definition and disqualifying half the essays. How will you ever learn anything if you do that?"

"I guess," I admitted sadly, "that I won't."

"Well, you'd better look at them with new eyes."

So I tried. I discovered how complex, once we move into the realm of creative suffering, the variety is. Just as, two generations ago, William James opposed the common assumption that there was some single kind of "religious experience" and wrote *The Varieties of Religious Experience,* so it now seems to me that there is no one "creative suffering," but many different kinds. And there seem to be so many kinds precisely because there are so many levels and capacities of the spirit. Just look at some of the experiences we have read about in this book!

We have learned of Frederick Franck's struggle to overcome his "meddling, cheating ego" and to renounce his free choice, which is referred to as "the sickness of the mind." The suffering that he experiences is a unique separation of himself from himself. Only as he separates himself from himself and gives up his "ego" is he able fully to identify with "fellow creatures, with landscape, with city, sun and rain," so that these other beings may now live through his drawing. I now feel my first impression of Franck's essay was completely wrong. It seems to me that his experience has a Christlike mediatorial quality. The artist, by giving up his own being, makes it possible for others to have their being through him.

But how different from Franck's, even contrary, is the experience described by Charles Davis! His suffering involved not the separation of himself from himself, but the integration of himself with himself. In his difficulties, Davis felt a growing obligation to be true to his own conscience, a growing obligation to make a personal decision to sever himself from the historical community in which he found himself. From this decision, he discovered a strange paradox—that aloneness is the way to a new kind of community. "The suffering inherent in the lonely responsibility of personal decision is creative inasmuch as it creates community." Only, I would phrase it: As a person is absolutely true to himself as he is, will he be able to be absolutely true to others as they are.

It is striking that although the psychology of suffering seems to have been very different for Franck and for Davis, the outcome of that suffering seems for both to have been very much the same. Whereas Franck's suffering involved the separation of himself from himself and the giving up of his free choice, Davis' suffering required the integration of himself with himself and the affirmation of his freedom. But both discovered as the result of their inner travail, a new dimension of personal life. They discovered a new oneness with other beings, a oneness whose mark it is to accept others for what they are.

As we move to McKenzie's essay we are in a new world. Of the private anguish described by Franck and Davis, McKenzie remarks that this is hardly fit topic for discussion. His personal experience of suffering within the church involves, evidently, no sense of self-dividedness or struggle with himself, and there is no evidence that its outcome is a self-transformation or the experience a new dimension of life. The suffering McKenzie experiences is the pain and indignity inflicted upon him by the McIntyres, Krols, and Cushings. And he justifies his endurance of this kind of treatment by reiterating, in self-defense, that "I gave as good as I got." ("The few occasions on which I failed to reciprocate are still a bit distressing.")

Moreover, it is striking that a mode of suffering, even culpability, that affected Davis deeply does not bear on the conscience of McKenzie. Davis felt a deeper degree of identification with the church than McKenzie does. And this is why Davis felt it was "an evasion—'bad faith' in Sartre's sense—to disclaim interest in and responsibility for the official corruption of the body" to which he belonged. So Davis left. McKenzie, on the other hand, does not seem to feel united with those who represent the church if they make decisions with which he disagrees and which cause him suffering. By his very act of disagreement, he feels himself separated from them. His sense of what it is to be in the church is utterly different from that of Davis. Though McKenzie believes in the unity of the church, he does not *experience* the consequence of that belief in his own inner dividedness.

Martin Luther King felt so united with all other men that he refused to return violence to any man. I said, "Refused." It would be more accurate to say that he felt "spiritually unable." To do violence to others with whom he felt identified would be to do a further violence to himself. It would be to suggest that their injury to him was not also an injury to themselves. To know all men to be bound together in a spiritual brotherhood is only possible, of course, for the eyes of faith. But to return suffering for suffering inflicted is the fundamental act of faithlessness, the basic act of unbelief in the universal holy communion of mankind. This is why King calls every Christian to "willingly accept that violence upon yourself, so that self-suffering stands at the center . . . and may serve to transform the social situation."

Notice that the experience of suffering discussed by each of these persons varies precisely because the persons themselves differ "spiritually." Davis was more "bothered" than McKenzie about feeling one with the bishops in a historical community in which he had inherited membership. Hence he was spiritually unable to remain in the church. He didn't *choose to leave*. Having the kind of spiritual attitude he did, he was *unable to stay*.

To the extent that Davis now belongs to communities, he feels they must be voluntary ones. In voluntary communities he can feel unambivalent and authentic because he has chosen them and can affirm the decisions and behaviors of the other members—no matter what they do. Were these other members even to cause him harm, he could, in principle, affirm and accept their action without retaliating. For example, his marriage is such a voluntary community. It is not just a theory, but a matter of common experience for all of us, that to "repay injury for injury" to those with whom we are one flesh is not simply to hurt them back, but to hurt *ourselves and them*. In such a case, nonviolence is the natural consequence of a spiritual feeling about a relation to another. One who fully loves another does not simply *choose* to suffer evil at the other's hands rather than to retaliate. One who fully loves another is simply *unable* to retaliate.

To develop this principle farther, if the community to which a man feels he belongs is the spiritual brotherhood of *all* mankind, he will live a totally nonviolent life. This was the experience of Martin Luther King, a man who not only went through the lonely decision to separate himself from all inherited communities (to be a *man* and not just a *black*), but who then reaffiliated himself with every other man in spiritual brotherhood by an act of faith. If all men are brothers, then—King knew—the injury they did to him they were also doing to themselves. That is why he believed no injury requires repayment. For every injury injures the one who inflicts it as well as the one on whom it is inflicted.

A man who feels this way about the spiritual brotherhood of man not only does not repay violence but is unable to do so. He is, quite simply, a greater and more dignified being than the one who acts violently against others. Violence is, so to say, alien to his person—for he feels, as part of his integrity, a oneness with all other men. What I am suggesting is that creative suffering makes possible the growth of the human spirit and the emergence of new attitudes, feelings, and motivations. These new attitudes and feelings are so integral to one's identity that to take hold of them is, quite literally, to become a new person. This was certainly Paul's experience when he spoke of the new attitude and motivation of love and freedom that was formed in him after his meeting the risen Christ. He called these new attitudes "Christ living in him."

But let us approach this matter from a nonreligious standpoint. John Galbraith, in *The New Industrial State,* points out that different societies are organized in terms of different motivations and attitudes toward life. In a very primitive society, the fundamental motivation of men is the sheer avoidance of pain—*compulsion*. A more complicated society can replace the threat of pain with another motivation—*the promise of reward for work performed*. We might call this the "profit motive" (though the gaining of status, or power, or being on the winning side are also among desired rewards). To replace the threat of pain with the promise of reward is not only to have a different motivation, it is to have a different kind of person. Persons motivated by promises have a large inner life because to respond to a "promise" requires a greater degree of *self*-motivation than to respond to the threat of immediate bodily pain.

Galbraith points out, however, that yet a third motivation is dominant in highly developed societies—*the motivation for sharing and identification*. For certain kinds of persons—those who feel that the meaning and integrity of their lives is not in themselves alone but also in other men whose company they love—the motivation of sharing and identification is greater than the desire for mere profit or reward. Such people help their friends, not for payment, but for the pleasure of their company. A society which can build on this motivation of identification, therefore, has within it people whose capacities for personhood are larger and more generous than the capacities for personhood associated with the first two motivational types.

Finally, Galbraith notes, there is a fourth motivation—*adaptation*. This motivation leads a man to identify with others and share their lives even though they do not requite him with friendship and the joys of common life (that is, the values involved in the third motivation). A man might be willing to forego this return because he has a faith and vision for others toward which he hopes to help them grow. He might, for example, be willing to endure their violence against him because he seeks—through his nonviolent identification with them—to help them gain a vision of the brotherhood of man. His motivation—in Galbraith's terms—would be *adaptation*. Persons who can act in terms of this motivation are simply greater in spirit than those who cannot.

We see, then, that Galbraith's analysis of motivations is nothing other than a nontheological way of discriminating different "sizes of spirit." The man who acts because of the promise of a reward is a larger, more fulfilled person than one who only acts because of the threat of pain. The man who acts because he finds joy in community achievements and seeks to share his life with others is a larger, more generous person than one who acts only because of a promised reward. And a man who, like Martin Luther King, is willing to share the common life and to seek to identify with even those who wish to destroy him is a still greater kind of person. The motivations and attitudes that produce his nonviolent, caring response in all situations is evidence of a magnitude and dignity of personhood which is the goal of every man's struggle to grow spiritually.

This spiritual growth is the end for which man has been created, and the suffering that is creative is the suffering involved in this process of spiritual growth. Suffering assists the spiritualization of man, that is, *some* suffering does. Actually the mere endurance of suffering is valueless in itself, and can even be a defense against spiritualization. For example, there are husbands and wives, priests and bishops, teachers and students who play out—day by day—a ritual of mutual aggression as a defense against having to face the childish and destructive tendencies in themselves. This is not creative suffering, but destructive. Another example of destructive suffering is the pattern of blaming others for doing things that you yourself are doing to them—using the excuse that they did it "first," or that they are bad while you are good. Yet another example is the destructive flight into the "safer kind of suffering"—as when we prefer to suffer the loss of our freedom as a less risky alternative to having to make decisions for ourselves. Another kind of destructive suffering comes by our displacing our fears and angers into our bodies (which then become ill) rather than our courageously confronting these fears and angers for the sake of becoming well.

Suffering is creative only as it leads to the growth of the human spirit, to man's becoming like God, to sanctification. It is creative because it leads to the discovery of new dimensions of reality and new forms of personal life. Physical suffering is not, therefore, the highest suffering; rather, the highest is spiritual. It is in the spirit that the growth toward larger and more generous forms of personhood takes place. And it is more painful to suffer in the spirit—to struggle for "the separation of self from self" as the larger and more generous you is being born. This is why the traditional Christian preoccupation with the suffering of the body—suggested by the symbol of the crucifix—so often leads us wrong.

Think of the matter this way for a moment. Which

do you think was the harder thing, which do you think involved the greater suffering—the crucifixion of Jesus or his passion in Gethsemane? Was the greater pain in his giving up his body to God while on the cross or his giving up his soul to God while in that midnight garden?

Isn't it really the case that we ordinarily assume the worst suffering is that which is endured by the body because we have never faced the harder kind of suffering which a man endures voluntarily in the dark garden of his soul? We assume so easily that the hard suffering is that which is inflicted on us rather than that which we voluntarily choose—the thorns which are placed on our head rather than the thorn we freely grasp and hold in our hands.

But can there be serious question that the harder suffering is that which takes place at the inner center of the soul, and that it is harder in part because we must endure it in solitariness and voluntarily? We must choose to grasp this nettle and endure its pain alone. Only in our *voluntarily* dying to ourselves in the aloneness of our own spirit can God live in us. The greatest suffering is, therefore, not of the body but of the spirit. This is why it cannot be *seen* by others.

The endurance of bodily suffering, the suffering that can become a spectacle and be praised as "heroic," is only of value as it makes possible an experience of the spirit. Thus the crucifixion of Jesus is of value only as it gives us evidence of the reality of Gethsemane. The two thieves who were crucified beside him also endured bodily suffering, and they may have endured this pain as heroically. Where, then, was the difference? It was in this: Jesus was there because he had, through the suffering of his spirit, given up his own will and become one with the will of God. It might better be said, therefore, that Jesus' "true crucifixion" happened in that solitary garden and that what happened on the cross was only testimony to what had occurred the night before.

This is why, I suggest, the Christian does not see any value in bodily suffering for its own sake. The enduring of bodily suffering is only of value to the extent that it affirms the reality of spirit. This is what voluntary bodily suffering does: It confounds the superstitious belief that the sole reality and sole causes of things are those that are seen with the eyes and felt with the hands. It evidences the power and the presence of the human soul.

John Howard Griffin, in his essay, gave us a moving example of the way bodily suffering can teach us the reality of the spirit. He recalled for us Raïssa Maritain's sickness and her observation that her suffering involved the "faculty to act at once on two planes—that of concrete experience, demanding and painful, and that of an abstract and liberating conception rooted in the same experience." Because suffering can give rise to this experience of twofoldness, of acting at once on two planes, the endurance of bodily pain can give testimony to the reality of the spirit. Alan Paton also called attention to this same twofoldness when he observed that those who refused obedience to unjust South African laws invited suffering but also witnessed to an invisible realm of divine justice and creativity and thereby encouraged the endurance of others.

In such twofoldness—whether it be the struggle of

our soul against the disease and timidity of our body or the struggle of our emerging "oversoul" against our soul —there is always the pain of a growing self divided against itself. There is the pain of separating from certain narrower, less generous forms of living and reaching upward to identify with one's higher self. To grow through suffering in this way makes possible a certain carefree indifference to the concerns, the values, the ideas of one's childhood. "When," noted Alan Paton, "Francis of Assisi got down from his horse and embraced the leper, he solved the problem of suffering for himself." He solved it because he knew that that part of him which could be inflicted with leprosy was not the source of his life. He solved it because he knew that something he once had been, he was no more. A certain growth, or spiritualization, had taken place in him. He had, through inner struggle, put aside his childish self and become a new being.

Frank Sheed, in his essay, rightly reminds us that the teaching of Christ was not simply a doctrine, but a redemptive and healing word. In the same way, he points out, the truth we believe must not be mere knowledge of events and doctrines. It must be a truth that spiritualizes, a truth that sets us in motion and causes us to grow. If it does not do this—but simply becomes a fortress to be defended or a weapon for attack—it is not Christian truth. Christian truth must become the spirit of love, the power of more generous personhood, in those who affirm it and believe.

How is this to occur? Primarily, Sheed says, the truth grows in men "by being lived, prayed; obeyed, disobeyed; doubted, found good; rejoiced in, suffered in. A truth thus in operation is seen with a clarity that a truth simply heard or read cannot have: it becomes an organic element in the men who live it."

I find these words eminently wise, eminently sane. They recall to us things we must always keep in mind: Every truth about God must head us *Godward*. Whatever suffering comes from him must make us more *like him*. And, in me and in you, these things can already be under way.